Advanc

M0000I3323

"*Road to Hope* touched my heart at every level. I smiled. I cried. I laughed out loud! I felt all the feels—the loneliness, pain, fear, strength, exhilaration, and joy—right alongside Dena. In fact, I found myself in her story. Dena's heartfelt memoir inspires every seemingly 'ordinary' woman to embrace the messiness of change so that she can free the extraordinary woman within. *Road to Hope* reminds us that we are all on this journey together—the journey to discover who we truly are, shed the layers of who we thought we were supposed to be, and love ourselves with compassion and grace. *Road to Hope* is not merely a story. It's a roadmap to help each of us live a more meaningful, authentic life."

—Sarah Elliott, Entrepreneur, Executive Coach and Founder of the
Ellivate Alliance

"*Road to Hope* is simultaneously enlightening and empowering. Dena Jansen speaks with such clarity and authenticity and encourages us to step into vulnerability as an accessible gateway to growth, courage, healing, and transformation. This book is like a best friend that reminds us that we are not alone when it comes to connecting with the deepest parts of ourselves and living our lives to the fullest."

—Paige Davis, Entrepreneur, Author of *Here We Grow: Mindfulness
Through Cancer and Beyond*

"With grace and charm, Dena Jansen tells a story that we have all heard from our girlfriends. Grab a glass of wine and make room on the couch because Dena only does it in a way that makes you cry with laughter while teaching a powerful story of inspiration. You will see yourself in her stories and feel like you've been there all along. *Road to Hope* is perfect for women making transitions in life or wanting a booster shot of confidence."

—Terri Broussard Williams, Founder, MovementMakerTribe

"Any woman going through a time of transformation should read *Road to Hope*. Each chapter felt like a parallel to my own life, and it meant a lot to read such an honest recount from a woman that worked hard to find her path. Being along for Dena's journey helped me better understand my own and show me that we don't have to feel alone along the way."

—Madeline Pratt, Founder and CEO, Fearless In Training and Womxn Talk Money

"What I love most about this wonderful book is that Dena has captured every man and woman's journey through life. Almost all of us follow the expectations of society, parents, religion, and peers and become someone that we are not. As we awaken, we realize that we can only be truly happy when we find and embrace our authentic self. Anyone that struggles with that gnawing feeling of inauthenticity (and don't we all) will find *Road to Hope* to be a valuable guide on their journey."

—Michelle Chalfant, Founder, *The Adult Chair*

"Dena's story teaches us one of the most profound lessons in life and one we need to hear often. Everything happens for us, not to us. Her bravery and vulnerability inspire us all to rise above fear and live our best adventure!"

—Carly Pollack, CCN, MS, Owner of Nutritional Wisdom, Author of *Feed Your Soul*

"Dena provides her own raw and authentic journey that many women can relate to as they are mid-career with young children and have demands at work and at home. She shares her own story of how, when feeling despair, rather than running away from it, she instead dug in and decided to learn, while utilizing the community around her to lift her up. I believe *Road to Hope* is great for career-driven women that 'want it all' but haven't taken a moment to pause and ensure they have defined what that means in their life and whether they are intentionally living the life they desire. By joining Dena and her life story, you will find practical guidance along the way to help you with your own."

—Amy Vetter, CEO, The B3 Method Institute

DENA JANSEN

ROAD
to
HOPE

How One Woman Went from
Doubting Her Path to
Embracing Her Inner Journey

This book is a memoir. It reflects the author's present recollections of experiences over time. Some names and characteristics have been changed, some events have been compressed, and some dialogue has been recreated for storytelling purposes. Some dates and events may not be in the exact order that they occurred.

For information about this title or to order other books and/or electronic media, contact the publisher:
Dena Jansen
getinspired@denajansen.com

Cover and text design by Sheila Parr
Cover images © iStockphoto / RayTango, Shutterstock / Zakharchuk
Author photograph by Leandra Blei
Author photograph hair and makeup by Marisa Warren

ISBN paperback: 978-1-7340713-0-6
ISBN hardcover: 978-1-7340713-1-3
ISBN ebook: 978-1-7340713-3-7
ISBN audiobook: 978-1-7340713-2-0

First Edition

For JoAnn

Contents

Introduction: *How Did I Get Here?* 1

Chapter 1: *Passion Lost and Found.* 9

Chapter 2: *Hurry Up and Prove It.* 25

Chapter 3: *Voices and Choices* 35

Chapter 4: *Childhood Curiosity.* 53

Chapter 5: *Focus and Fear.* 67

Chapter 6: *All the Feels* .85

Chapter 7: *Poolside Epiphany.* 97

Chapter 8: *Let Go and Let Life.* 107

Chapter 9: *Campfire Clarity* 119

Chapter 10: *Teamwork Makes the Dream Work.* 137

Chapter 11: *Goodbye and Thank You for Coming* 155

Chapter 12: *Signs Along the Road* 171

Chapter 13: *Life Goes On.* 185

Chapter 14: *I Have a Dream.* 193

Chapter 15: *Peace, Love, and Comfort.* 207

Conclusion: *What's Next?.* 223

Acknowledgments. 229

Introduction

How Did I Get Here?

I'M SITTING IN MY CAR, hands gripping the steering wheel. There's no one else around. It's dark and foggy, and the traffic lights dangling above me are blinking red. I'm at a familiar intersection of two county roads surrounded by open fields. The high school I went to is down the road after the big curve to the right and the baseball fields where my son played tee ball are down the way to the left.

During the day, this traffic light is backed up with cars and construction as our small town continues to grow. But after 10 pm or so, the town feels sleepy. The roads are near empty, and the traffic lights go to blinking as everyone is tucked in safely at home.

The red light keeps flashing off and on. I know what that means. I'm supposed to stop before proceeding through the intersection with caution. But tonight, everything is blurry and out of focus. I've forgotten what's in front of me. I don't know what to do. I'm stuck.

My heart begins to race. Dread creeps into the car alongside me, but beyond that, I'm completely alone. I don't know where I am or where I'm going. I'm lost. Engine idling, I'm stranded at a crossroads.

I wake up to realize it was only a dream. I know this feeling though; I'm familiar with it. I've sat at an intersection like the one in my dreams before—stalled at a real-life crossroads in my life. Alone and afraid.

Over a matter of years, darkness and doubt slowly crept in, leaving me unsure and unsettled in my life, my marriage, and my career. And after stalling out multiple times and nearly wrecking everything, I finally grabbed hold of a life-saving truth:

I had a choice to make. I could stay still and stay stuck, or I could try and find new roads that would lead to the peace and joy I was looking for.

I don't know if it was desperation or a glimmer of hope that helped me choose which road to take, but ultimately, I decided the only way I could move forward was to look at my life from a different perspective. To take a step back and try to understand the choices I'd made up to that point in my life. To really look at the behaviors I'd clung to and the relationships I was in. To see how they all merged together to create the woman I'd become.

Now, you might be wondering, *Who are you, Dena?*

Well, allow me to introduce myself. I'm a small-town girl from Buda (pronounced Byou-duh, not Boo-duh), a suburb south of Austin, Texas—the same area where I was born and raised and continue to call home. I've been a wife for over 18 years, married at 20 to my high school sweetheart. I've been a mother for more than 12 years, and my two babies are a constant source of pride, joy, and parental frustration. I'm a Certified Public Accountant. Yes, that's right a CPA who spent 15 years as a number crunching and rule following auditor.

Who I am *not* is equally straightforward. I'm not famous. I have no following. I've been no hero. I didn't climb any giant corporate ladders.

I'm pretty simple—a plain-Jane some might even say. I like my small town, my favorite local Mexican food restaurant down on Main Street, and the fact that I can get to a Target in under twenty minutes.

And I have to admit, at the time I was idling at that crossroads, my life probably looked great from the outside looking in. But even though it looked great, somewhere down deep, something was missing. At the core of my being, I was unhappy and unsettled.

Don't get me wrong, my life journey was one I could look back on with pride. I'd been responsible and loyal and gotten my job done, whether that was at work or at home. I'd made choice after choice, including some hard decisions along the way. I didn't have regret, except that at some point I had stopped being curious about how my choices impacted me and my quality of life.

I had shifted into autopilot mode and lost conscious control of my life until, at 36 years old, I looked myself in the eyes and wondered:

How did I get here?

That question came with sadness and defeat. And the answer—*I have no idea*—was one that I could no longer accept. I finally realized that somewhere along the way into adulthood, wifedom, and motherhood, I had failed to stop and ask myself one fundamental question:

What do I want?

As I focused on my roles and responsibilities as a wife, mother, and professional, the question of what Dena wanted wasn't a top priority. What did my babies want? What did my husband want? What did my team and clients want? Those questions I asked myself frequently. But what did *I* want? Well, that question felt foreign.

Pause for a second and ask yourself the same question:

What do I want?

Feels strange, doesn't it? For years, I hadn't asked myself that question, and I don't remember anyone asking me. And my guess is that it's the same for you. But as I mustered the courage to sit with myself and give the question the time and attention it deserved, here's what came to mind.

I wanted to love and be loved. I wanted to feel and share feelings with others. I wanted to laugh and cry. I wanted to think and learn. I wanted to speak and be heard. I wanted to make a difference in people's lives and know that my life mattered.

Those longings are what started my journey of self-discovery and growth nearly four years ago. When I look back on where I started, my heart still hurts. I was hope starved, isolated, and losing energy every day. I'd become a mere shadow of myself, and I'd never felt so alone. I knew what I wanted: a happier and healthier version of me. But I didn't know how to get there.

And I feel confident you might have some of these same feelings.

I think you picked this book up because you want to feel enthusiastic and energetic about your life, but you can't seem to find your way there. You have all the pieces of the puzzle—marriage, kiddos, career—but when you put them together, you still don't feel whole. There must be missing pieces, but you can't find them. You wonder why you can't make it work when so many other women appear to be able to do it so effortlessly. And so you give in and get stuck in a roundabout of doubt.

I'm here to tell you I have been there. I've been stuck in that same gloom and doom loop. And the only way I got out was to get in my own way.

While I was starting to figure out where exactly I wanted my life to go and the best route I should take to get there, I realized that me, myself, and I was the only place to start. For the first time in my life, I had to make it all about *me*. Being the center of my own attention was something I was apprehensive about off the bat. But I had to focus on myself. I had to try all the things that I thought mattered to help me create the life I said I wanted.

And you will have to do the same thing.

At the time, I didn't see my journey as part of a more significant movement—one of feminism or female empowerment. But looking back, I can see how it was part of a rising tide. Maybe you have felt it, too. My 70-year-old aunt always said to me, "You girls these days. Y'all just don't settle."

She was right. All around me there were strong-willed women pushing for more in their own lives. Like them, I believed that I was meant for more than what I was at the time, and I wasn't going to settle until I searched out exactly what that more was.

Navigating through my life the last few years has been an adventure. Learning how to get back in the driver's seat of my own life felt like learning how to drive all over again. At the beginning, I needed lots of direction. I made some wrong turns and found dead ends. But the more experience I gained behind the wheel—the more knowledge and confidence I developed in myself—the more equipped I became to try out the freedom these new lanes opened up for me.

So before I speed off into the sun-kissed horizon toward the life of my dreams, I owe it to myself to spend time in true reflection. To look back in the rearview mirror at the living and learning that occurred on the road all over again. To honor the amazing growth and healing that happened along the way and share it with the next brave woman looking for hope.

And my gut tells me that woman is *you*.

I want to share my journey with you. You can sit right up here next to me while we wander the roads I traveled. Please take anything you need from my story that might help you in yours. I know that our lives might not look exactly the same from the outside—different home and family situations, career paths or trajectories, personal successes or struggles—but I genuinely believe that our dreams are very much the same. We share dreams of deep love and connection in our marriages, our families, and our work.

And we desperately want those dreams to become our realities. But in order to make those dreams come true, we have to get on the road and go. We have to go and find ourselves first.

But I'll be honest with you. While I was out finding myself, I also found that the road can get lonely. That's why I pray you'll take the risk and hop in the car with me this time. It would give me a ton of comfort to know I had a friend alongside me. That the words I'm sharing won't go into the darkness, but rather, find you right where you are in your own journey and give you the hope you'll need to keep going.

I've grown from a woman who was lost and alone to one who is confident and ready for the next adventure. I want you to experience that exact same shift. And more than that, I believe you can. But first, I can't wait to tell you how I got here.

Are you ready to hit the road? I know I am.

Buckle up, friend, and enjoy the ride. I know I did.

Chapter 1

Passion Lost and Found

ARE YOU A PASSIONATE PERSON?

I ask because much of my story has everything to do with passion. No one ever asked me that exact question, but it's an important one. One that I wish someone *had* asked me.

If someone had asked, maybe I would have realized that passion was exactly what I wanted in my life, but didn't know how to define. I wanted to feel alive, steady and sure that my life and the things that I cared for and about mattered. That's how I understood passion. Passion was fuel for a life that mattered. I didn't have words to put to the basic human need of "mattering" I was longing for most of my life, but that was what I wanted—what I will always want. And I bet you want the same thing.

So before we dive into my journey, it seems only right to fill you in on some run in's I've had with passion over time, almost

36 years' worth of time to be exact. And time is such a crazy thing isn't it? Minutes drag by, but weeks, months, and then years fly by leaving us wondering where all the time has gone.

And for me, and I bet you too, there were a few moments in life that we remember as if they were yesterday. There are other moments though, moments where we made big life decisions, where we had a choice to make that would alter our life's path that we can barely recall. Regardless of how clear the memory is all the moments mattered.

But when you combine the time that is flying by and the constant call for decisions to be made, it's easy to see how we get off track when it comes to pursuing our passion and personal growth. I was no different, and as I look back in my rearview mirror I can piece together moments when I wondered, learned, experienced, and then eventually lost the life-force that is passion . . . that is, until I found it again.

I will never forget the day. It was a bad day in early spring of 2008. I was sitting in the therapist's office. My mother-in-law, Peggy, sat outside patiently holding my six-week-old daughter, Elizabeth, in her arms. I was sad to be back in this place because I'd been here before—and "here" was the painful void of postpartum depression.

I experienced my first round of postpartum depression with my son, Trace, a couple years earlier. I battled the emotional and physical disconnect in those dark days. Waves would roll over me—waves of anxiety, nausea, and prickly, creepy-crawly sensations worked up and out from my gut and over my entire body for months. Sometimes I couldn't sleep, lying awake in bed for hours. Other times I couldn't sit still and gave into pacing aimlessly.

But what I thought were dark days with my son were only a fraction of what I experienced with my daughter. The first go-round might have been waves, but the second was a tsunami. For a matter of months, I was almost unrecognizable.

I was lost but determined to find help. Therapy had been my personal cry for help the first time through. So as soon as postpartum symptoms started up again, I knew I needed to head straight to therapy for help. That's when I found Dr. Maynard.

I didn't go with intentions of digging into my life; I just wanted him to fix me and make me feel normal again. And together, we tried it all. I took all the pills that he prescribed and continued to come back for weekly sessions of talk therapy with a glimmer of hope that we'd find the fix to heal whatever was broken.

After several sessions, I was still feeling way off, actually getting worse. I felt small in the middle of the big couch. But maybe today would be the day. We were having the same conversation we'd been having about how to connect to myself and my family and not be emotionally erratic. No matter how much we talked about it, I was still emotionally unnerved and physically restless.

"When will this end?"

That's all I wanted to know. I wanted answers. After a long pause to consider my question, he responded:

"Maybe you just aren't a passionate person."

The answer must have made sense to him, but it threw me off. It was like Dr. Maynard had reared back and sucker punched me straight in the gut. I couldn't breathe. I was sitting on the couch, but inside, I was hunched over and gasping for air. My heart was hurting, and my soul was pleading against what felt like a horrible accusation.

No, you can't be right. I'm passionate. I have feelings. I love my family, I love my husband, I love my children. I'm just sick right now. I have passion. I care about things. I have some reason for being here and alive. Surely, I matter.

I said some of those words out loud to him then, willing him to take back what he'd said and agree that I had passion. But he didn't take back his words. And as I walked out of the office, I took the exchange we'd had and etched it in my heart and mind.

After a couple of long, grueling months, I gradually regained my emotional footing and fell right back in line with my family. It had been a rough patch, one I was glad was behind me.

While my postpartum symptoms eventually faded, I've never been able to shake that moment on the couch. And as I neared my thirty-fifth birthday, the question of passion remained.

Was I a passionate person?

What is passion anyways? And how do we find it? When I

thought on the question and looked at my children, I came to the conclusion that we learned passion at an early age. It was something wildly unique. My son was an outdoor boy. He wanted to hunt and fish and play all day, every day. My daughter enjoyed crafting, creating, and Netflix. They had polar opposite passions.

My children wouldn't use the word passion to describe themselves or what they loved to do. And I wouldn't have used it as a child either. But even though they aren't saying it, I do believe they have experienced and internalized the spirit of passion, just like I did as a child.

You see, I believe every person has had some moment during their life when something lit a fire in their soul.

Mine was in fourth grade. I was 9 years old in Mrs. Wilke's class. She had given us an assignment to select a historical figure to research and present to the class. I picked Martin Luther King, Jr. My parents took me to Blockbuster, and I checked out the "I Have a Dream" speech on VHS.

I put the cassette into the VCR and watched it. Then I watched it again . . . over and over and over.

"I have a dream . . . I have a dream . . . I have a dream today!"

I was in awe of the power in his voice, the feelings he made me feel, and how my body reacted with a racing heart, goosebumps, and tear-filled eyes. At 9 years old, I couldn't fully understand the reality behind his calls for actions and the struggles of a society that didn't treat all as equal. But I understood dreams. I understood hope. And for the first time, I understood passion.

As an adult, I tried to think back on that first moment where I fell in love with a powerful speech and speaker. That first moment I recognized passion. Of course, I didn't run out and start speaking to crowds and inspiring the masses like MLK. But I had connected with something, even if I didn't know what to do with it yet.

And maybe that's just how passion ebbs and flows. We keep growing up, learning as we go, and trying a new thing here and there to find our passion.

For me, that new thing was leadership. Dr. King was a leader. And I started to see that same quality in myself. I liked to lead. In middle school and high school, I was drawn to being part of and leading student groups. People joked that I was President of everything, but they were kind of right; I was!

As I prepared to head to college at Texas Tech University, I decided to major in something that seemed to make the most sense to my super mature 17-year-old self: business management. I liked businesses and I liked to manage things, so it made sense. But after only one hour of Business Management 101, I decided I had to look for something else because it was so boring. There had to be something more interesting—something to be more passionate about.

At the time, I was also taking Accounting 101, and while lots of people felt like that class was equally boring, I found it came pretty naturally to me. Believe it or not, it was fun! Nerdy as it seemed, it was exciting to me when things added up and agreed. Plus, the graduate assistant teaching made big promises.

"You will always have a job if you get an accounting degree."

I would always have a job? I decided right then and there that I was in. Sign. Me. Up.

In that moment, I made my first unconscious choice between passion and practicality. While the numbers made sense to me, I never stopped to ask myself if a career centered around that fact was my passion. The answer might have been, *I don't know.* The real loss was not having asked myself the question in the first place.

After graduation, I found that my accounting degree had, in fact, landed me a job right out of college and promised me a career with no end in sight. I was over five years into that career on that fateful day when Dr. Maynard gave me the one-two passion punch. But the passion I fought for that day in his office was in no way connected to my work. During those first years in public accounting, I quickly realized that I was not deeply connected or passionate about my work. I sat in my cube and got my work done. But mostly, I sat with another coworker as we dreamed of what else we could be doing for a living. While his dreams were all about grilled cheese, mine weren't as clear.

And just like that, another eight years of my life and my career passed by in a flash. I had moved from a national firm to the largest locally owned and operated CPA firm in the heart of downtown Austin. As far as places to work go in this industry, it couldn't get much better.

While I loved the firm I worked with, that nagging feeling that accounting and auditing weren't what I really wanted to do with the rest of my professional life remained. Every day I was less energized and excited about what I spent so much of my time doing. But the flexibility and financial stability my work afforded me made it hard to consider other options.

After a few years at the firm, I was asked to consider a promotion to partner. While that should have been an exciting offer as the final step up the corporate ladder, I was hesitant and asked for time to think about it. As part of my soul searching, I sought guidance from other partners and executives in town and found the messaging was consistent: They believed I was ready, they'd support me even if I messed up, and regardless of my decision, they'd love me.

One executive shot me particularly straight.

"It sounds to me like you are a scaredy cat. And you should never make any decision solely based out of fear."

Fear was certainly playing a role. Fear of messing up, fear of bringing down the firm, fear of not having the answers that a partner should have. More than that though, I was reckoning with a fear of commitment to the role and what it meant for me long term. How could I agree to be a partner if I had a very clear sense that I didn't want to stay in this profession forever?

I took all the information I'd gathered. I talked it over with my husband, JP. I talked it over with myself. It was an opportunity to learn and to grow, and it wasn't a decision that required me to sign my life away. So after one final check for consensus, I found that we all felt I should go for it! I let the firm know, and transition plans began.

One year before my partner transition, I joined a three-year emerging leaders' program. It was a new program to me, but from day one, I was excited about the personal growth and leadership topics. I found myself intrigued by the books I was reading and new conversations I was having.

The two men leading the program kept saying that they wanted us to become change agents. They encouraged us to find our strengths, hone in on them, and put them to work. They challenged us to raise our hands and use our voices.

"Raise your hand!"

Simple as that seemed, the physical act of raising my hand and inserting myself into a conversation was intimidating. It was hard, and far too many women, including me, were holding ourselves out of the action because we wouldn't make the first move. We wouldn't push our hand up in the sky. Instead we kept our hands nicely folded in our laps and missed huge opportunities to contribute.

Armed with their challenge to first take notice of how I was engaging in my new role as partner, I quickly realized that in many meetings, I had in fact gone quiet. I had given into silently weighing the cost of looking like a fool over the cost of making an actual contribution. This internal debate usually ended with me saying *something*, just not *all* the things I truly wanted to say.

But after that leadership course, I decided I had to go for it. I started raising my hand. It was a first step towards the pursuit of passion. One that every woman must take. I was nervous the first few times, but then, I started to feel the energy that came from contributing my ideas. If becoming a change agent meant raising my hand, I was definitely doing my part. My arm was a lightning rod sending down little bolts of energy straight from the sky down through my bravely raised hand.

So I let the energy keep rolling. I started offering to speak and do presentations on things that excited me—personal development and people skills rather than standard and traditionally dry technical topics. It was then that the stirrings started. Nagging little thoughts and ideas about what I might really want to do with myself and my career. Every single time the recurring thought that came to me was that I should speak.

I decided to act on my inkling first in front of the people I cared about most. I threw my name in the hat and was given the green light to do a presentation entitled "The Power of Dreams in the Workplace" at our annual firm-wide meeting. It was the first time I shared pieces of both my personal and professional stories with my coworkers. And honestly, I loved it. Time seemed to fly by and stand still at the same time as I breezed through that presentation. It felt amazing, and after talking with a few people and hearing that they connected with my stories on a personal level, this inkling that speaking might be my passion was confirmed.

I had reached a conclusion. At a very high and dreamy level, I knew what I wanted to do: I wanted to speak. Speaking and sharing in front of a group of people was my happy place. It was my passion. I'd found it again. Or maybe just reconnected with it when the time was right.

Unfortunately, discovering your passion is only half the battle. Figuring out how to make it happen is a whole other thing! When I would talk to my husband about it, he always had a couple of fundamental questions.

"Okay, Dena, what are you going to speak about?"

"I don't know."

"Who are you going to speak to?"

"I don't know."

So I didn't have all the specifics figured out. That was fine. My heart knew where it wanted to be. And the fact that I was willing to voice it to myself and my husband was a brave first step.

But that first step was about all I could take toward my dream at the time. I was committed to learning my new role as partner. I'd found my passion project in speaking, and I wasn't going to let it go ever again. But I still had work to do.

About a year and a half into my role as partner and during my final year of the emerging leaders' program, I was completing one of my program assignments to talk to a client about something other than work. True to the assignment, I brought up my desire to speak. My client said, "Well, then you should meet this guy I've worked with. He is a great speaker and coach."

I was all about adding someone new to my network, so I set up a time to meet him. And when I did, I found the work he did to be fascinating. His work was focused on the individual—who they were, what they were about, how they brought their passions to their work, and how that all translated to the experience others had with the person.

He offered a full day coaching session that sounded intriguing. It took me a couple months to muster up the courage to actually commit. My dragging feet were due to a healthy dose of fear; I was scared of exactly what I would or wouldn't discover in the process. Ultimately, I chose curiosity and courage over fear, and I walked into the day both nervous and excited.

I will forever call that day my Discovery Day. I walked in

with a few things in addition to sweaty palms and a racing heart. I came with a genuine desire to learn something. An open heart and open mind ready to explore. An honest spirit that knew it didn't have answers or clarity on this speaking dream but was still prepared to search for them.

But I also came in with a lot of apologies. Yeah, that's right, I had a chorus of, "I'm sorry" to offer. I had an unusual habit of apologizing—one that I'd never noticed before. Apparently, I'd answer a question and then apologize. I'd ask a question and then apologize. Then I'd apologize for apologizing.

Once my coach noticed it, he started a freaking tally on the board. Watching another tick go up each and every time I said, "I'm sorry." Well, it was annoying and embarrassing.

Why was I so dang sorry?

Apologies are used to express regret or remorse for something that you've done wrong. And I knew I wasn't saying or doing things that were sorry-worthy. I wasn't intentionally harming anyone. Somewhere down deep, did I think there was something wrong with speaking my mind? I had to find a way to believe the answer to that question was a firm and confident, "No!"

That simple exercise of self-awareness was first of one of many game changers for me. It helped me see a pattern—one that was no longer serving me. I was able to become aware of my unconscious apologizing and decided to change my ways. I'm proud to share that to date, I've banished the habit of apologizing from my everyday conversations. Sorry, guess I'm not sorry anymore.

I think that somewhere down deep there was a part of me that felt like I should have stayed put and kept my mouth closed. That one part of me was sorry to all the other parts of me for taking time out from my real job that day—from my usual roles of partner, wife, and mother—to spend time learning about the woman I'd become. *How dare I?*

But I couldn't stop just as I was getting started. A part of me that I didn't recognize well held firm to an unspoken fact that I was worth my own time. It was okay, even more than okay, it was necessary, that I not apologize for pursuing self-discovery, buried passions, and ultimately, hope. That part of me somehow knew that if I stopped, I would be missing out on the most important adventure of my life.

So even with all the reasons it felt selfish, investing in myself and Discovery Day also felt awesome. And was that really something to apologize for? No, it wasn't. It was something I should have been thanking myself for! To have one person solely focused on *me*, prepared to help *me*, ready to believe in *me*? That was a treat! And it was one I deserved.

I never thought that I'd walk out of my Discovery Day seven hours later with such a sense of clarity. I came out with answers about what I could speak about, the story I had to share, and who I could possibly share it with. Those answers sparked a light in my heart and soul.

My excitement was so palpable that at one point my coach asked me, "Where do you think all this is coming from?"

"I just know I'm meant for more."

He wrote the declaration that flashed to my mind and out of my mouth on the board.

MEANT FOR MORE.

Those three words solidified all the other words on the board. In that moment I believed I had a destined purpose in life. I had an active passion to pursue. And I believed there were other women out there who were like me—women who dreamed of more for themselves. I wanted to find those women and encourage them to find the bravery to dream and the courage to strive for continual growth in the same way I was going to try to do.

Scribbled all over the whiteboard were the initial ideas of what my dreams could look like. Something new was born that day; it was a true soul awakening. Along with the clarity I found on what my message would be, I also found a real and tangible sense of hope. Hope that I could actually do the thing that I'd been longing to do.

I sat there high on hope and stared at the whiteboard full of ideas and words—words that looked to be a real-life road map to my dreams. Still in shock, I asked the coach, "How did you do this? How did you come up with all this?"

"I didn't. This was all in you. I just helped get it out."

I was having a hard time recognizing and celebrating my contribution to my own discoveries. I was quick to give him both thanks and credit for the words on that board, but the reality was that the work was actually all mine. I was so grateful for his guidance, but I was going to have to learn how to be proud of myself for plotting my own course.

Discovery Day was a gift. It changed the trajectory of my life. Not only did I have a dream of speaking and inspiring others, but I also now had knowledge and information that told my logical brain I could make those dreams a reality. I had natural talents and a message that I thought the world needed to hear. I could do it . . . if I wanted to. I had a choice.

As I walked to my car and headed home after Discovery Day was done, I found that my brain was nowhere near done. I couldn't sleep that night. In fact, I went sleepless for days. My heart and mind raced with energy and possibility. I had reclaimed my passion. The questions, ideas, and dreams were running wild and free. But there was one question that I'd been challenged by so many years ago that I could now answer with certainty.

I *was* a passionate person!

And my soul was wide awake.

Chapter 2

Hurry Up and Prove It

"YOU NEED A PROOF OF CONCEPT."

That's what I wrote down when I sat with a woman I'd never met. Still amped up after my self-proclaimed soul awakening, I was eager to connect with anyone who'd talk to me about how the business of speaking worked. That morning, I was sitting across from a woman who was touted as a successful business owner, author, and speaker. She was a bit older than me and retired from a successful career as a corporate executive.

I was a bit intimidated when we met. I felt that my professional story did not come close to the one she described. Self-employment and entrepreneurship were new concepts to me. I had no idea how to start a business. Still, I tried to be all ears. I shared a bit, but mostly, I asked questions and took notes. And when we went our separate ways, I focused on one nugget she'd shared.

I needed a proof of concept. I needed some way to prove that my Meant for More way of living made up of all those words on the whiteboard on Discovery Day would translate to real change. I needed proof that finding the bravery to dream again and daring to strive for continual growth could really cause actual humans to edge closer to happier and healthier versions of themselves, their relationships, and their careers.

I had to prove that it worked for me so that others would not only believe it could work for them, but hire me to help them do it one day, too. Figuring out how to do it became my top personal and professional priority. I needed proof, and I needed it now.

The search for my proof of concept gave me exactly what I didn't consciously know I needed. I hadn't known what my next step should be in my professional pursuit, so I was thankful to be armed with a new task to check off toward this newfound dream of mine. It gave me something to focus on while I tried to gain some sense of control over my potential transition. Aimlessly wandering made my blood run a little cold, but latching on to the task of proving a concept allowed my brain to step in and lead my heart.

It didn't take long for me to piece together a plan that I thought would surely lead to success. On Discovery Day, I'd done a self-assessment on how strong I felt in five areas that my coach called pillars of self-worth: physical, emotional, intellectual, spiritual, and passion. The exercise was intended to help a person evaluate all the areas in their life. Higher ratings in each pillar implied higher levels of inherent self-worth. What if within six months, I could increase my ratings on that self-evaluated, self-worth exercise?

The exercise and concept of self-worth aligned nicely with my Meant for More mission of continual personal growth. Back on Discovery Day, I had rated myself 1–10 on each pillar, with most categories falling between 6 and 8. Not too bad, but definitely room for improvement. That was my starting point. Then at the end of six months, I'd rate myself again. If my ratings went up (which surely they would, right?), I would prove that I'd increased my level of self-worth, and then, my overall life satisfaction, joy, and happiness. Genius, right?

But how would I actually raise my ratings? My analytical mind stepped in with a plan. I would seek counsel from people who I thought were already higher rated than me in each pillar. People that I respected and who I felt had something more of what I wanted—physical strength, emotional stamina, intellectual prowess. I'd bring them into my fold and surely their higher rating would somehow rub off on me. And because I was a goofball, I would call them my Pillar Peeps! Because who doesn't like a little alliteration to keep the party going?

I recognized these people as experts in a particular pillar, and I wanted their help to bring me up a couple notches. With their support as my personal board of developers, I would share my real-life journey with them and explore lots of new things over a matter of months. If it all worked like I planned, I'd prove out all the concepts that I'd dreamed up and become a happier, more fulfilled human along the way. Gosh, it seemed like a good plan.

With that in mind, I started to eye out my Pillar Peeps. I had laser focus and a belief that the Universe would send me a sign so I'd know exactly who my Pillar Peeps were meant to be. In real life, that meant I combed Facebook and made mental and emotional connections to the people I scrolled through. The Universe gave us Facebook, right? Why not use it to help me stock my plan with people? Once I'd created my list of potential Peeps, I reached out and took my prospects out to coffee or lunch to share my new professional dreams and proof of concept plan.

Some were new acquaintances; some I'd known since grade school. I told each one that I thought they had something special to teach me in their respective pillar. Then, I asked each one if they'd help me by stepping in to the role of Pillar Peep. Each one said yes. Looking back, they were all probably wildly confused by exactly what I was asking, but they all agreed to support me nonetheless. Truth be told, I didn't know what I needed, but I was willing to try and learn on the fly. Layering other people into the plan seemed to automatically increase the odds of my success.

Who were my Pillar Peeps? Well, the lineup included a super fit friend from high school that I'd reconnected with, another high school classmate who now had a counseling practice, an intellectually charged editor-in-chief that I knew from my childhood church, and a soul-singing new acquaintance with an incredible personal journey of faith. They were a motley bunch that I pieced together after a few easy gut checks and Facebook messages. These people would make me better. I just knew it.

But as the days and weeks passed by, my killer plan started to fizzle out. I had asked the Pillar Peeps to help me, but I didn't know what to ask them to help with. I was darting all over the place with no real idea of where I was headed. In my planning, I failed to recognize that these were people with their own lives, families and careers. They didn't have time to drop things and guide me. *Duh, Dena. Why hadn't you thought of that?*

With my Pillar Peeps plan feeling more and more like a failure, I had no idea what to do next. Just like that, I started to feel lost all over again. I woke up every morning and kept going to work, dreaming of possibilities and somehow expecting my trajectory to magically change course by itself. My ratings weren't going anywhere, except down with my sinking attitude. The plan wasn't just failing, I was. Frustration set in as there was no noticeable change. After all that planning, somehow I was still stuck.

Guess I could have pulled over and stopped the car right then and there. Life was getting hard and the new thing I was trying wasn't yielding fast or amazing results. I could just stop and decide that it was a dead end. But something in me realized that even though this plan wasn't working, something else might. I couldn't give in when the going got just a bit hard, for the first time, I was seeing that quitting would have been the real failure. I needed to keep going, keep seeing what I could learn.

But instead of slowing down to get my bearings and trying to figure out exactly what I wanted and needed to learn, I kept seeking out more people. I was eager to connect to new acquaintances with ideas and experiences that fed into my passions for personal growth and entrepreneurship. My network was expanding to include folks in human resources, coaching, consulting, and speaking. I'd been in the numbers business, but

I needed to know people in the people business. And they were all good people with kindness and wisdom to share.

"Yeah, it's scary, but you can do it, Dena."

"You'll love the freedom you have when you're out on your own."

"People need to hear what you have to say, Dena!"

These people were giving me exactly what I hadn't realized I had been looking for from my Pillar Peeps—caring attention, guidance, and lots of affirmation that my dreams mattered. These were human needs we all have—love, connection, growth—and they were needs that I had not been fulfilling in my own life. I didn't know that as a fact then, but I certainly felt its truth at the time.

Each new meeting gave me an addictive boost of energy. I was connecting to people, learning so many new things, and it made me feel so alive. It gave me that windows down, hair blowing in the wind, singing to my favorite song while flying down the highway kind of excitement. But sometimes that's the danger of speeding down the highway. You're so caught up in the excitement that you don't see clearly what's ahead.

That's just what happened with one relationship that evolved into something more than professional support and mentorship. One of my new business colleagues that I'd met early on in my exploration started to provide me with more than a kind ear. He was confident and curious, and just like that, I was drawn in.

There was a sense of intensity when we were together. An entrepreneur with passions for people and growth, he'd done things in his life that I was only dreaming of doing myself. Yet it was easy to share with him where I was in my professional journey—something I was struggling to do with my husband at home.

While my husband might have easily rolled along with me as I considered a speaking career, he was having a harder time with the idea of me actually pursuing a life of self-employment. JP and I knew the ebbs and flow of working for yourself since he'd done it since graduation. My career kept our family stable and insured. There were six figures in my salary that were scary to think about leaving behind. So instead of traveling down dark road conversations like those with my husband, I went somewhere else—somewhere there was light.

It was easy to talk and dream of endless possibilities with this other man. We had no history together. No present-day realties to consider. No real risks to stare in the face. Instead, he embodied a new future. And on top of that, he was all ears. He asked me questions, he listened, he threw out things for me to consider, and he made me feel like he believed in me and my journey. He made me feel special.

Unfortunately, I wasn't able to recognize then what was going on inside of me. I had intense human needs underlying all of my wants and dreams, and my unconscious desire to fulfill those needs was starting to take over. I felt the pull to change careers, but I was also longing to feel the pull of love and connection, growth and contribution, and even moreso, some excitement in my personal life.

My life outside of the office had become predictable. And my Meant for More journey was opening the door for me to explore what my life could look like outside of my career—how it might look different and, even better, more exciting. Even though I longed for something new, I had a deep desire to still feel safe and sound. I was scared of staying the same and scared to try new things. I was pushing my gas and my brake pedals at the same time, going nowhere fast. Again, I was stuck.

Eventually, the thrill of the unknown pulled just a bit stronger. And I leaned into the more exciting space where the woman I dreamed of becoming was welcomed. For me, that space was with this other man. Over a matter of months, I built him up in my mind, gave his words priority, and allowed our time together to mean more and more to me. What started as coffees turned into work meetings before turning into text messaging and phone calls. What began as professional conversations turned into personal ones, including talk of our spouses and marriages.

The lines of what this relationship was about got blurred, but it was harmless. That's what I told myself. Sure, there was an energy between us, and it made me feel alive. But that was as far as it went. That's what we told ourselves. We were so bold as to even talk about the attraction we felt. We prided ourselves on the fact that we hadn't acted on it.

How adult of us, right?

How could this kind of friendship hurt anyone? Now I see that as a simple question with a very easy answer. It could hurt people deeply because marriage is built on trust. And while there was never any infidelity in any physical way, emotional connection and attachment with someone other than your spouse is harmful to that foundation of trust. That was something I was unable to recognize at the time.

I couldn't recognize it because I'd been stuck for so long and wanted to get unstuck. I was focused on who I wanted to be—I wanted the greener grass and I wanted it now. But in my haste, I got sidetracked which so many of us do. We get so focused on the dream that we give into convincing ourselves that anything is true as long as it keeps us moving towards what we want. That's when rational thinking often times goes out the window.

The relationship quickly became an invisible emotional crutch for me. My Meant for More journey wasn't only a professional one any longer; suddenly, it was very, very personal. I wanted to be happy again, and it seemed that when I was with him, I was. With him became the place I wanted to be because that is where I felt like the woman I wanted to be—a confident and capable woman.

Thinking back on it now, the whole thing was like a mirage. The relationship, the connection, it all seemed so shiny off in the distance. But I had no way of knowing if any of it was real. I could barely keep myself from heading toward it though. A moth to the flame. We'd only known each other for a matter of months, but I was allowing myself to trust his words and his direction over all others.

My husband, on the other hand, a man who I'd known since I was fifteen now, seemed like he had less and less to offer me. I was creating all new story lines for our marriage. *He doesn't understand me. He doesn't care to. He doesn't support my dreams.* And I was buying into them myself. If only I'd been able to recognize that it was mostly the work of my ego longing to feel cared for and safe. If only I'd realized that I wasn't as emotionally equipped as I thought I was. Maybe I wouldn't have gotten so far down a path that was getting harder and harder to turn away from.

But where was I on my path anyways? With only a few months left before my self-imposed deadline for my proof of concept, I found that not only was I still a bit lost professionally, but now I was also lost in a personal crossroads that I hadn't seen, or more honestly, hadn't wanted to admit was coming.

I had been so focused on trying to run and force my way through the unknown in my professional path that I had forgotten one simple fact: You can't separate the person from the professional. I was one human with one heart and soul guiding me along my life journey. I was one human that was about to truly live and learn the old saying that you have to walk before you run.

Sometimes that walk was headed straight toward something, and, at others times, it was walking away from things that needed to be left behind. Regardless of the direction, I was about to learn that I couldn't rush change. I couldn't ignite my passions overnight and think they might not burn me or those around me. I would have to put one foot in the front of the other, ever so slow and steady.

Right foot, left foot. Right foot, left foot.

One. Step. At A Time.

Chapter 3

Voices and Choices

"HE DOESN'T THINK YOU HAVE ANY HOPE, DENA."

She didn't follow it up with a question like, *Well, do you, Dena? Do you have hope?* She—the woman on the other end of the line—was my mother-in-law, and the "he" she was referring to was her son, my husband. This woman loved her son, but she also loved me. She even told me so moments before when I answered her call. I cried when I heard her say those three words because they were true. I cried because she was hurting, my husband was hurting, and I was hurting. I cried because our marriage was hanging on by a thread.

"I've seen this before, Dena. If one person doesn't have hope, it's over."

I had to ask myself the important questions.

Was he right? Had I lost hope?

Days before she'd called me, I probably would have said he was right. And that thought led me to one more question:

How did we get here?

I met JP our sophomore year in high school, and the rest was history. It was crazy to think that we had been a couple for more than 20 years. We never broke up, never took a break. Nope, no Ross and Rachel moments for us. We were babies when we met, and we literally grew up together. When people heard we were high school sweethearts, they either responded with surprise or told us how sweet it sounded. Regardless, we didn't know it any other way. It was just our story.

After high school, I followed him to college where he played football at Texas Tech, and only a couple of years later, he asked me to marry him. Engaged at nineteen and married at twenty, we started our grown-up journey together. The first trip I ever went on without real adults along for the ride or paying the tab was my honeymoon.

Were we ready? Capable and responsible, yes, but not completely equipped. Were we scared? I can't answer for him, but sure, I was. We were smart though and could figure this marriage thing out. Fake it 'till you make it, right? How hard could marriage be?

We both graduated with our college degrees and headed our little butts back home. Going home was never a question since farmland doesn't move. My hubby was a farmer and knew he wanted to be from the time he was a little boy. He grew up with farming on both sides of his family, so he found his passion for growing things early and held tight to it.

JP's a strong, willful, annoyingly disciplined and loyal man. He's also a super handsome, tall drink of farm boy water! He's determined and competitive and works hard to get what he wants. According to him, he knew he wanted to marry me from the first time he met me.

We created two precious children, a son and a daughter, and we've been pretty good parents doing the best we can to raise them to be good humans. They are a funky mix of our DNA, our personalities, our faults, and our gifts. We remain proud of them and love them with all our hearts, but we also know that they'll most likely have their own therapists someday to help fix all the things we did as parents to screw them up.

As great as we might have looked in a family portrait, what people didn't see was that we had been struggling. There wasn't one event or one hard year where it all began. We had lots of good times and great memories; we had the pictures and Christmas cards to prove it. But as our professional lives got busier and the kiddos demanded more of our time, it was a slow-paced deterioration that neither of us was emotionally equipped to identify, let alone brave enough to deal with in a healthy way.

We slowly began to allow life to pull us into its predetermined paths as if we were operating on autopilot. In the same way a person can individually lose conscious control, so can a couple. The paths we mindlessly went down made sense, and we didn't have to think too hard along the way. It was, "you work,

I'll get the kids," tag-team parenting, leaving little time for any focus on ourselves or our relationship.

I found my antidote to unhappiness and my seemingly disconnected marriage in busy-ness or isolation. I ran around managing the kids and their lives when I wasn't working to keep myself busy. JP on the other hand found his reprieve in work, work, and more work. We didn't take time to check in ourselves or with each other, never asked if we were happy with ourselves or each other, and rarely fought. Both of us simply kept moving, avoiding each other even if unconsciously.

Neither of us reached out or spent much time with friends. We'd become isolated and apathetic within the walls of our home, cordial to each other mostly but not genuinely kind or caring. Instead of putting in the required effort to connect, we remained silent and created storylines, assumptions, and patterns of behavior built on years' worth of unexpressed anger and resentment.

Just as I had started to toy with the idea of a new career, I also finally started to admit that I was desperately lonely inside our marriage. But things really started to change after Discovery Day. *I* started to change. I was getting braver, more curious, and was determined to find a new path in my professional life—a way that would lead me towards my dreams of more joy and fulfillment.

The ripples from my professional soul awakening spread into my personal life. I began to actively question everything about my husband and our marriage. *How did we get here? Is this how it will always be?* And while I was running toward new ideas and new people on the work front, at home, with all these unsettling questions, I started pulling ever so slowly away from my husband.

With the personal growth spurt I was experiencing, I found it hard to explain all that I was thinking and feeling to JP. When I tried to communicate something new I was learning, it wasn't met with the same excitement from my husband. I was fresh and full of passion outside of my home, yet I started to feel the need to dim my newfound enthusiasm when I was inside my home.

I began creating all sorts of stories in my mind about his reactions or non-reactions to things. I walked around with all sorts of assumptions about what he must be thinking or feeling. But instead of asking him in the moment what he was actually thinking, I chose to keep all my doubts and fears to myself. I began harboring beliefs that he either didn't care, didn't believe in me, or even worse, that he didn't understand me and might not ever again.

I was eager to travel new roads. I saw myself charging ahead, ready to grow and evolve. I wanted him to grow too, but he seemed content to stay on the same roads of status quo. I was beginning to see a "new" me surface, but with those new eyes I found myself looking at the man I'd grown up with as if he was a stranger. This new dynamic not only frustrated me, it also sparked a light of fear for what this shift might mean for us long term.

The unspoken tension kept rising between us until it became loud and clear one weekend that started with a six-hour car ride to Lubbock.

JP and I remained virtually silent for the duration of the trip. Even though there were no words, my mind was racing.

We were in town for a fun family weekend we'd planned and were staying with my best friend and former college roommate, Alisa, and her husband. As soon as we arrived, I quickly cornered my dear friend in her bathroom. (Don't private conversations feel safer in private spaces?) I sat on the edge of her bathtub and spewed out all the words, questions, doubts, and fears that had been piling up over the last few months. It was like a floodgate had been opened, and I let it all out.

"What if JP won't ever understand me again? What if I've never loved him at all? What if I'm not attracted to him now or never was? Why does JP even love me? He doesn't seem to need me. I feel completely disconnected, and I don't know what to do."

I had kept all these fears to myself and not shared them with anyone. In the darkness of my mind, they had turned from small doubts into huge questions. And I know I'm not the only woman who has allowed her mind to take over and create scary storylines and false mental narratives. We hold so many thoughts in the corners of our minds too scared to share, too fearful of the emotional exposure. But we forget that the only way to find out what's real and true is to let it all out and shine some light onto whatever it is we are holding on to so tight.

When I finally finished, exhausted yet satisfied from the emotional purge, Alisa had a question of her own.

"D, why didn't you tell me?"

My response came back quick and clear. "Why didn't you ask?"

Those two questions repeated themselves in my mind as the day passed by.

Why didn't you tell me?

Why didn't you ask?

Why in the world had I assigned her the responsibility to ask me? To somehow manage me and my life? Who had given her the job of reaching out to make sure I was taking care of myself and my relationship with my husband? Whose life was it anyways? It was mine. My life. My marriage. My decision to retreat from family and friends and avoid dealing with a relationship that was not healthy. Those were my choices.

Even though I still had so much to figure out about my marriage, I knew there was something about that moment that I had to take hold of. Something inside me told me: *You need to learn this now, Dena!* So, I did. I had to choose to reorient my thinking going forward. I would have to take responsibility for my own reality. I would have to take ownership and ask for the love, help, and support that I needed from that day on. I couldn't wait for anyone to do my life's work. Period.

I wasn't the only one asking questions that weekend. Even though he hadn't said it, I knew my husband felt the crack widening in our marriage that weekend, too. And as we waited outside one of our favorite college restaurants, JP looked me in the eyes and asked one simple question.

"What do you love about me?"

He'd already rattled off a few things he loved about me, but in that moment, I couldn't come up with an answer.

My eventual response? "I'll have to think on it."

The tension was thick and rising, and both of us knew it had to be close to overflowing. But as we'd grown accustomed to doing, we let the moment pass and went about the rest of our time in Lubbock as if everything was fine.

But it wasn't fine. I woke up the next morning feeling sick. For the six-hour drive home, I stayed silent, my face buried in a pillow while my mind and stomach churned. The 400 miles we drove across Texas that day felt brief in comparison to the miles we still had between us. I couldn't shake the nausea, so I put myself straight to bed once we made it home. My daughter left a note on the door.

"Mom you need to feel better now!"

I agreed. I wanted to feel better, but my heart and head were all tangled up. I didn't know how to process the fact that I couldn't respond to what should have been an easy question: *What do you love about me?*

As we were lying in bed a couple nights later, I finally felt well enough to discuss his question.

"I'm ready to talk about your question."

"What question?"

Fire rose in my belly as the words, "What question!?!" spewed out of my mouth.

He stared at me blankly. I blasted back that I guess he needed time to remember. I flipped over and away quickly, angry and hurt at what felt like a blatant attempt to avoid the mess that we were so deep into now. My heart burned and my mind raced, knowing that we were going to bed with important words left unsaid.

But before I turned off the lights, I mustered up one last bit of courage and tried to hold to the lesson I'd learned: I had to take responsibility for my reality. My back to him in bed, I faced what I saw as our reality and asked for what I thought we needed.

"Whether you remember your question or not. We need to talk. Can we do that tomorrow night?"

"Sure."

The next night, after the kids were in bed, we met in the living room to start the conversation that we'd agreed to have. Scared and awkward, we sat on opposite sides of the couch, not knowing if we needed to be close or far, far apart.

JP held a pillow in his lap, maybe as a sort of buffer as he sat back reclined in the chair. I sat with my back straight and resolute. The conversation weaved from side to side, but never went off the road. We both stayed calm. And no matter what, I wanted to make certain things clear.

"We aren't good, JP."

I told him that I wanted to feel like he was growing with me. That I was scared he wouldn't. He didn't reassure me that he would or could; instead, he just sat there, looking me in the eyes.

Then, he asked his own questions. Questions about me and my new acquaintance—the man who was coming up more and more in conversation. JP had started to sense that I was attracted to the other man's presence. He knew that the other man was in the mix of my frustration with him since I had expressly compared the two at some point. Up until now, he had used humor to maneuver around the issue—even joking that maybe I'd left my shoes at his place a few nights back when I couldn't find them. But now, he wanted to know more.

"No, nothing physical has happened between us. Have you ever been attracted to other women?"

He shared a story of a one-time run in at a bar with a woman when he was away at work. He might have had a few drinks, and she very clearly let him know she was available.

"I was all by myself," he explained. "I knew you would never know if I did something. But I knew I couldn't do it. I just couldn't do it. I never could, Dena."

There we were, literally asking each other if we'd been faithful. These were questions that I never thought I'd be asking myself or my spouse. But now, we were. For hours, our words covered the distance between us—sharing fears, frustrations, and feelings we'd never shared, asking questions we'd been afraid to say out loud, trying to start a dialogue that we'd never really had in all our years together. And the main question that remained that neither of us said out loud was simple:

How did we get here?

How did we not see the walls we'd built around ourselves, keeping the other person on the other side? They'd been built, brick by brick, layer by layer, by the choices we'd made. They were held tightly together with the glues of fear, silence, and isolation. How did we not see them coming? How did we not notice once they were there?

After several hours, we'd finally run out of words. But we still didn't have any answers. Feeling the need to close the distance, I asked if I could come and sit near him. He nodded his okay. Then feeling like the awkward teenagers we once were, I asked one last question.

"Should we sleep together or go to separate rooms?"

The answer that felt right to us was to sleep—or at least try to sleep—together, side by side.

The next morning, we woke up feeling bruised and broken. We had hit rock bottom and were struggling with what to do next. After JP went to work with the same bloodshot eyes I'm sure I had, I got out of the shower to find several screens full of text messages from him.

"I love you."

"I want you to be happy."

"Do whatever you need to do."

My heart sank, interpreting the messages to mean that he had given up on me and us already. I had no clue what to do except grab my keys, get in my car, and drive the short five minutes to get over to my parents' house. I walked up to the door, knocked, and fell into my mom's arms sobbing as soon as the door opened.

She listened as I filled her in on all I could. She didn't have any idea we were facing these hardships because I hadn't shared the realities of our seemingly happy home. I told her for the first time what I had days before told Alisa—that I kept hearing a whisper in my mind. It was a hushed voice that I could hear saying, *Separate.*

Should we separate so we could work through all this? I didn't know. She remained calm as she shared some of her and my dad's own struggles, ones that I'd witnessed as a child but never thought of from her perspective as a wife and mother. She didn't give me answers, but she made it clear that she loved me and would support me and JP as we worked through things.

Mornings later, after several more tense conversations, JP kept asking questions of what would happen next. He was trying to make it clear that he hadn't meant for the texts to read that he wanted out. He didn't want me to go anywhere. I was the one who was wondering if I should stay or go.

"We aren't that broken, Dena. Things aren't all bad."

As he sat on the edge of the bathtub that morning, eyes red and swollen, I saw in him a deep pain and wild fear that I was partly responsible for creating. And it hurt like nothing I'd ever experienced. I'd never seen him look so lost.

"JP, I hear what you are saying. But I cannot guarantee anything anymore. I can't promise you that things are going to work for us. But I promise that I will keep coming back to talk with you every day as we make the next right decision."

Those few days were heart-wrenching and all-consuming. I was no good at work. I couldn't focus or concentrate. I was lost. One morning as I tried to get ready for work, I hit my own personal bottom—both emotionally and physically. I slipped and fell getting into the shower. I cut my foot and landed hard on my side. My body hurt, but it was nothing near the pain my heart was experiencing. So, I sat there, naked and hurting with the hot water running down my face. I gave in, allowing myself to be heartbroken.

And I sobbed.

After pulling myself together, I headed into work. The whole time, I kept hearing that same word—*Separate*—over and over in my mind. I trusted the word was there for a reason, and honestly, I kept thinking it meant I was to separate from my husband. Blocks away from the office, I called Alisa to try and figure it out.

This was a woman who loved me and had absorbed my bathtub download a few short weeks earlier. This was a woman who had kindly listened then and genuinely asked why I hadn't reached out before. I heard that message loud and clear and had decided from that moment on, I was in charge of seeking out the help I needed. So that's what I was going to do. She was my go-to, and God love her, she chimed in that morning with another dose of wisdom.

"Dena, what if you are meant to separate from someone other than your husband?"

As soon as she said those words, I knew what she meant. I had shared with her about the other man and our profession-al-turned-personal relationship. We all knew he was part of the messy picture.

Dena, what if you are meant to separate from someone other than your husband?

Why hadn't I thought of that? God, I loved Alisa. I thanked God for her presence in my life and the way she graciously loved me just as I was. She hadn't judged me or told me what to do. She loved me, and after fifteen years as friends, she loved my husband, too. She loved us both enough to tell me the truth.

Dena, what if you are meant to separate from someone other than your husband?

What if she's right? What if I was supposed to separate myself from a man that I had become emotionally invested in who wasn't my husband. I was coming to realize and admit that the relationship was not healthy for me or my marriage. JP had made it clear that he wanted us to stay together and figure things out, but he'd also made it clear that for us to move forward, I had a choice to make.

"Dena, I want us to work through this, but for that to happen, he has to go. He can't be part of the picture if we are going to move forward."

He was fighting for himself and our marriage and knew we had to focus on only the two of us to do that. But there was a new part of me that didn't want to just do as I was told. I wanted to make this decision on my own.

That's where I was in my heart when I heard those words from my mother-in-law.

"He doesn't think you have any hope, Dena."

I let them soak in, knowing there was a choice to be made. Did I have hope or not? Did I believe that my husband and I had potential or not? Could we weather this storm and come out stronger, happier, and healthier together? Could we learn new ways to care for ourselves and our marriage?

Moments before she'd called me, I probably didn't believe any of these things were possible. Until . . .

Until, at that moment, I decided. I would choose to have hope. If I was a true believer in potential, how could I not choose to believe in us? We were worth the effort. We could be more than we were then, but it was going to take a lot of work.

We hadn't known how to verbalize the emotional disconnect we'd been experiencing until we almost separated and had to admit that we needed help. Now we were making a choice to stay together and work to find a better way. And we'd have to do all that work without knowing if our efforts would succeed. We'd have to choose to have hope and faith in our potential. We'd have to figure out how to make our marriage work again. We'd have to find a new way.

But before we could do any of that, I had to separate.

I picked up the phone and called the other man. With a shaky voice and anxious gut, I shared that JP and I had made some big decisions together. He remained quiet through most of the call, allowing me the space to quickly share what would be my goodbye.

"We admitted that we aren't in a good place and have work to do," I explained, "but we are committed to trying to figure things out. I'll be forever grateful for your impact on my life."

With confidence and sadness, I told him that having him in my life was no longer healthy for me or my marriage.

"It has to be an immediate and total sever of all ties. I don't want to have any contact. I have to focus on myself and my marriage."

His response? A short and simple, "I understand, and I'll respect that."

And he did. I never heard from him after that day.

After having to break up with someone that wasn't my husband, life seemed to get fuzzy and clear all at the same time.

How had I gotten here?

I'd asked myself this question before. But now there were more. How had I eased into making decisions that didn't align with the person I thought I was? I had become emotionally intimate with another man, and I had gotten freakishly close to crossing lines that aren't meant to be crossed.

Holy crap! What had I almost done?

Regret and the need for forgiveness took hold of me immediately. And one night as I lay wide awake next to a sleeping JP, I started where I knew I had to. I asked God to forgive me for the choices I had made and the pain that I'd brought into my marriage. I asked for help as we moved forward. In those quiet night hours, I meant what I prayed and was certain I'd been heard.

The next morning, I had to ask for the same forgiveness from JP. As much as I wanted to blame him for the state of our marriage and what had happened, I had to take the punch to my own gut. I had to acknowledge that I was the only one responsible for my choices. I had not been true to myself or our marriage, and I needed him to know I was truly sorry. I couldn't expect him to forgive and forget, but I prayed he would know I was sincere. I was so sorry that my choices had hurt him. I told him as much as we stood together in our driveway during the gray morning dawn.

It was just another morning to some, but for us, it was a morning I'll never forget. I was weighted down after taking ownership of my decisions. I felt the disappointment of what seemed like failure on several fronts. Here I was, only a couple months into in my six-month plan to have a finished proof of concept of my Meant for More way of living—the project I'd stocked up with Pillar Peeps and a ton of reckless naivety—and I had no evidence to show that it worked at all. Zero, nada, zip.

In fact, instead of my life getting better, it had almost fallen apart. I had tried to quickly plan and force my way into what I wanted and found out the hard way that I was going to have to slow my butt down and take this growth journey step by step, day by day, with faith that it would all fall into place.

My very own life experiences had given me evidence of other things though. I had proof that I was going to have to actually live out my Meant for More way to truly learn it for myself. I had proof that I was going to have to walk this new path slowly, maybe even alone at times, in order to see it to the finish. At others, I'd need to hold my husband's hand as we trudged forward together. I had proof that while I was not in control of the outcomes I hoped to experience in my life, I had to take responsibility for all the choices along the way.

Most importantly though, I had proof that life came down to choices. And it wasn't just for me, life came down to choices for every single woman. And we had to realize that every single choice was another opportunity for us to make a decision with the best information we had available to us each moment. We had to choose what feels right to us without worrying what anyone else might choose. We had to continue to make choices for ourselves, believing that our life's work is to create the life we long for—one choice at a time.

And we had to make choices with the ones we chose to be in relationship with along the way as well. JP and I had chosen each other years ago, and now, we picked each other again. We decided to give hope a chance, and I prayed that hope would rise back up and into our marriage. But nothing was guaranteed anymore.

Instead of focusing on "as long as we both shall live," every morning became an opportunity to choose all over again—to believe in ourselves, our marriage, and the fact that we were worth the effort it was going to take to get our lives back on track. Even though we couldn't see where the road in front of us would lead, we had the opportunity to choose to hold onto faith and our commitment to fight the good fight.

Together.

Chapter 4

Childhood Curiosity

SHE HAS A LAUGH THAT I WOULD DO ANYTHING to bottle up just to have available to hear on demand.

It's a laugh I've come to know well over the years, as it belongs to my friend Sarah, who I've known since middle school. She and JP shared the honor of being voted "Best Smile" our senior year in high school.

And that night, her laugh was the thing I needed to hear the most.

Sarah and I were eating dinner and catching up as I shared about mine and JP's recent come-to-Jesus meetings. As I opened up, she laughed knowingly, eventually letting me in on the fact that only maybe a year or so into their marriage, she and her husband had found themselves at a similar fork in the road: stay together or go separate ways. She explained that it had been heartbreaking, but at some point during all the turmoil (and thanks to a lot of time with her therapist), she had a realization.

"I just knew that I'd be okay."

Sarah's comment wasn't super wise or profound. She didn't say it with a ton of fanfare, but it still hit me hard. She had a moment where she knew that whatever happened, she—her alone, with or without her husband—would be okay. I hadn't known it until she said it that way, but I was longing for that exact same feeling.

Even before JP and I hit our big 'ole bump in the road, I had been struggling to get to know myself as, well, just me. And now, after making a choice to stay together, finding the balance between focusing on "me" and "we" was something I still had to figure out.

Since my focus on "me" started on Discovery Day, I remained wildly curious about self-awareness—what I defined as being honest with myself about myself. And there was one thing I could be honest about: I was not yet in a place to share Sarah's sentiments. I sensed true love, self-worth, and confidence in her statement—things I longed to feel about myself. But in the days and weeks before and after my marital fallout, I kept asking myself the same question:

Who am I exactly?

If I couldn't say with confidence that I knew who I was, how could I know that I would be okay?

So, who am I exactly?

The answer seemed simple. I am Dena Mueller (pronounced like Miller). That's who I was. Well, had been at least. That was my name before I got married. Then I became Dena Jansen. But I was more than the last name I carried. So, what about Dena? That was who I was really curious about—just me.

This curiosity started to show up in the pages of my journal that I started shortly after Discovery Day. And one day in September 2015, just weeks before my reckoning with JP, this is what I wrote:

Realized I haven't been alone since before I was 15. I've always been in a relationship. Still thinking on what that means now.

The very next day, my thoughts continued:

Yesterday I wrote that I realized I've been in a relationship since I was fifteen years old. I woke up thinking about it. I drove into work thinking about it.

Then the song "*Somebody to Love*" by Kacey Musgraves came on the radio.

Cue me interpreting Kacey's lyrics as they relate to my life.

The song spoke to me differently today. It wasn't about finding another person to love. It was about finding out that I needed to love myself.

I realized that I have not ever really been on my own. I have been attached to someone, loving someone, or maybe wanting to be loved for so long. I never had anyone teach me how to stop and fall in love with myself.

Never.

Who is supposed to do that for us? Do we just figure out "who we are" over time and in our own way? If so, would I know what I want, what I don't want, what I need, what I don't need? So many stinkin' questions. And I don't have the answers for myself.

And in all my years, I never stopped to ask myself those questions. I never allowed myself to experiment in life to get to know me. I just was who I was. I did what I did. I worked. I played. I married. I had children.

So, now what? I am a wife, a mother, a partner, a friend, a daughter, and the list goes on and on.

I realized today that I am meeting myself for the first time. Digging in deep and trying to decide for myself, without the aid of others, who the hell I really am.

One month after this entry into my journal, not only was I still trying to figure myself out, I was trying to figure out how to fix what had been broken in my marriage, too. My initial fascination with self-awareness had seemed like such a good thing. But if I was going to be honest with myself about myself, it meant that I had to face some things that weren't so great. I'd made choices that hurt my husband and my marriage. And having to see myself in a light that was no longer flattering, well—it sucked!

I'd broken the trust I had built with my husband. But I'd also fractured the confidence that I had in myself. I'd messed up and was having to remind myself that I could and would make healthy choices as I worked to figure myself out while also caring for my husband, our marriage, and our family. And while I started to work through it all—the "me" and the "we"—I realized that what my instincts had been telling me was right: My professional dreams had to take a back seat.

While it hurt my heart to take focus off of those dreams, a part of me knew something had to give. I could not do it all. I had zero capacity to give anything else focused attention. I was going to have to build my life back up from what felt like ground zero one brick at a time, and right now, I had to focus on the foundation—me and my family. I was determined that the speaking would happen one day, once we were stronger and ready to move on. I was not giving up on the dream. I was simply allowing myself the space to care for myself knowing when the time was right, I'd pick up where I left off. But for now, I had to slow myself down, breathe, and start reexamining my own life and the role I played inside my life and my marriage.

I quickly decided not to try and take on the role of self-diagnosing. I wanted help from a professional. I had worked with therapists before and it was time to return to a couch. After a few appointments, I found a new therapist, Jules, that was the right one. It was like Goldilocks when I found her. While other therapists before may have been too hot or too cold, Jules was just right!

Jules became a therapy mainstay in my life. She always gave me gems to chew on (Gems from Jules, as I called them).

"You can always dig!"

That was one of my favorites. Her comment was in response to my question about whether I should focus more attention on how my childhood might have impacted my life and relationships now—and not necessarily for the better. She never told me what to do; it was always my choice to dig in or lay off. But with her as my guide, I chose to slowly peel back the layers of my life.

I was ready to dig in.

❧

As part of Discovery Day, the coach started one of the exercises with a question: *What do you remember about your childhood?*

Honestly, I don't remember much. But you know what I do remember? I remember the night my dad didn't come home. I was in third grade, just nine years old. The same age as my daughter now. I remember knowing something was really wrong. My aunt and uncle were there. It was dark and felt heavy in the house. I remember going to find my mom in her room. She was sitting on the side of her bed. I asked where dad was, and she said everything was fine. He'd be home soon.

I knew she wasn't telling me the truth. I knew it. I went to bed like I was told. And when I woke up, he still wasn't home.

It may have been light outside, but there was a darkness inside the house.

My sister and I were sent over to a friend's house a couple streets over. We got word sometime later that morning that my dad returned home, but now he had to go to the hospital because he was sick. We made him a banner on the computer and waited for it to print out row by row by row on the dot matrix printer, slowly going back and forth, back and forth.

We visited him in the hospital. He was in bed with monitors stuck to his chest. He looked tired but not really hurt, no cuts or blood that I could see. From the outside, he looked okay.

This trip was the first of many trips to the hospital for the next 28 days. Twenty-eight days of what I'd later learn was detox and rehab as he worked to recover from his addiction to alcohol. Twenty-eight days of waiting for him to come home.

His room at the hospital felt cold and empty with only a bed, a dresser, and a Bible. We stayed with my aunt some during this time so we could get to school. But some nights, we'd go to the hospital and sit through these meetings where people stood up, said their name, and add on that they were addicts.

They'd share their stories, and some would get a chip. I didn't really know what the chip was all about, other than something to celebrate. At the end of the meetings, we'd all hold hands and say, "Keep coming back; it works."

The day my dad came home from the hospital, I got off the bus and saw him sitting in the swing that hung from a tree in our front yard. On the night he didn't come home nearly a month ago, he'd driven himself around for hours and didn't know where he'd gone. He made it back home that morning 28 days earlier, and now, he'd made it home again.

He was better. He wouldn't drink anymore. We'd taken out all the bottles of alcohol from the house. He wouldn't sit in his blue chair anymore, the one he always fell asleep in. We'd gotten rid of that, too.

The nine-year-old me knew that dad wasn't sick anymore, and she decided that she needed to do whatever it took to keep him from losing control again. Because if he did, he could die.

When I shared that memory with my coach on Discovery Day, he sat silent before replying, "Wow, it doesn't seem like you've healed from that."

Here I was months later, still wondering what healing really looked like. My childhood was so long ago; could it possibly still matter now?

And just like that, it dawned on me: Maybe it mattered a great deal.

Perhaps I was where I was because I'd never taken the time to get to know the little nine-year-old girl in me. The girl who had some of the same fears and needs that I now had as an adult. What if ignoring the jagged scars from my childhood had led me to create new wounds as an adult? What if my survival skills from childhood weren't serving me as well as an adult?

I wanted a healthy marriage. I wanted a healthy me. I wanted to be proud of myself for the choices I made and the relationships that I invested in. That's why I decided that I would stop and look way back at my life. Self-reflection seemed the only way to truly live and learn. If I didn't invest time in thinking back on my own life, who would do that for me? No one. And whether I was stopping to think back and reflect on my life a few moments or several years back, time spent looking for patterns of behavior was well worth it.

Who knew what I might find about why I did what I did or how I might be able to make slight adjustments to improve my life. Little nuggets of wisdom were waiting. That's why it felt necessary in order to take my next steps forward. I had to see if there was anything I could learn from my past that might help me change my future.

I became very curious about my patterns of behavior, when and where had they started and if they could change. One of the first books Jules recommended to me was *Struggle for Intimacy* by Janet Woititz. Once I started reading, I couldn't put the book down. It talked about the barriers of trust and intimacy that children learn in an alcoholic family. And I highlighted almost every other line in the book. I laughed out loud and made JP read pages that described me to a tee.

Seeking approval, isolating myself, avoiding conflict, stuffing my feelings. Check, check, check, and check. It was fascinating to see so much of myself in a book that had been written years back. It gave me a strange sense of relief. I wasn't totally screwed up. There were others like me.

Then, low and behold, as I sat in a meeting a few weeks later with a client that ran nothing other than an addiction treatment facility, it came up that my dad was a recovering alcoholic. After the meeting was over, one of the board members stopped me in the hallway.

"I heard you mention your dad. There's an Adult Children of Alcoholics group that I'm part of. If you are ever interested, you should join us at a meeting."

She left me her card. I had never heard of the group but was intrigued. So just like that, I was at their next meeting.

I only ended up going to a few meetings total, but I learned quite a bit in that short amount of time. Being the adult child of an alcoholic and growing up in what they called a "diseased" home brings with it a whole other layer of emotional complexities. I didn't end up liking to drink myself and never used drugs, but my need for control and approval from others were a few of the side effects that I personally walked away with from a childhood featuring alcoholism.

This, I learned, was called codependency. As a child, I'd heard the word in Alcoholics Anonymous (AA) meetings, but now, I was living it. Definitions of codependency include: addiction to control and approval or living in a way that thrives on the belief that, "I'm okay, really, only if, or when, you're okay."

Yeah, pretty sure I was a codependency addict.

I could see that I had a problem with latching on to others rather than standing alone. Not only had I clung to boys from an early age, but I'd also latched on to paths of least resistance, especially if someone told me it would be safe. Take my college major, the one that guaranteed me I'd always have a job, for example.

I could see that I avoided conflict like the plague and wanted everyone around me to be happy so I could say I was happy, too. My marriage and the way I tried to be a low maintenance wife were proof of that. I prided myself on it, actually. Over the years, I rarely told JP no when he was making plans. I didn't stop him from doing his thing. Because surely if he was happy, then I would be, too. Where had my avoidance of conflict gotten us? Nowhere in the end.

I was beginning to realize that by attaching my happiness to the happiness of others, I was no longer in control of my life. I had always heard in AA meetings or conversations about my dad's recovery that the hardest part for an addict is to admit they have a problem. And now here I was finding myself in the same boat.

When addicts admit they have a problem, they acknowledge that they are powerless over the effects of their addiction. They admit that their lives have become unmanageable because of it. Had my life really become unmanageable because of my codependency? Most people probably wouldn't have said that about me. It certainly looked like I had it all together. But they hadn't seen the story playing out behind the scenes.

I could look back and see it, though. Over the years, I hadn't rocked any boats. I'd made sure to stay in control—to stay safe and sound. I was a good girl, a rule follower. That nine-year-old little girl who learned that losing control could be fatal had guided me all the way into my adulthood.

I had lost control and made unhealthy emotional decisions. I had been lonely in my marriage and hadn't known how to seek the love I needed from myself or from my own family. For too long, I had avoided conflict with my husband, stuffed feelings so far down, chosen to live in denial about how far apart we'd grown. And when someone outside my marriage showed up and provided all the things I'd been lacking—connection, hope, and more—it was a feeling I couldn't resist.

At least until I decided that I must.

It was time to admit that I had a problem. I was no longer in control and needed to deal with my codependency.

One of the first changes I tried to make was to always look at my life through a lens of awareness. I wanted to stay curious about my own feelings, motives, and desires. Self-awareness was a way of being honest with myself about myself, even if it wasn't pretty. I knew that in my head, but now I had to make it a part of how I lived my life. I had to start asking questions. I had to keep asking myself questions—lots of questions.

Why did I do that?

Why am I reacting this way or that way?

Why am I drawn to this or that?

Questions that would help me look inside rather than outside for validation or approval.

There was another change I had to make, too. On top of self-awareness, I had to grab hold of self-accountability. I wanted to take conscious control of my life. If I was going to try and create healthier emotional relationships with myself and others, I had to admit that I was the only one in control of my choices. I had to remain willing to ask myself: *What do you want or need, Dena? And what are you going to do about it, Dena?*

I had learned this lesson already with Alisa and JP, but it was something I had to keep reminding myself of along the way. I had a personal responsibility to figure things out myself. I could no longer expect someone else to prompt me or push me to put one foot in front of the other. I had to try with all my might to hold myself accountable for my choices and my actions.

These weren't easy changes to make. Most mornings, I woke up flushed with anxiety. It was exhausting. Weathering personal storms and creating a consistent practice of self-exploration was a daunting challenge. But since I'd decided that no one could do the work for me, I knew I had to try something new to calm my nerves.

So, I decided to intentionally start my morning with just me. And then, God.

Every morning right after I woke up, I started checking in with myself. I'd take a pause to see what I was thinking or feeling. Then, I'd say a prayer. The prayer was always the same.

I recited the Serenity Prayer, a mainstay in the world of addiction recovery. I'd grown up knowing it, having heard it at the end of every meeting at the hospital with Dad. It had always given me a feeling of peace and a sense of closure. And while most people could say the first few lines, I repeated a more extended version. My mom had printed and framed in her house a version that had a few more lines that made the prayer feel complete.

God grant me the serenity to accept the things I cannot change,
Courage to change the things I can, and the wisdom to know the difference.
Grant me patience for the changes that take time,
Appreciation for all that I have,
Tolerance for those with different struggles,
And strength to live one day at a time.

Each morning, I gave myself attention. Then I asked God for guidance and support as I took slow and steady steps forward into unchartered territory. I still had way more questions than answers about who I was, why I did the things I did, and where I'd go from here. But I was starting to realize that answers naturally led me to more questions—more profound questions that would help me understand more about myself and my relationships.

I was choosing to trade my unhealthy addiction to codependency for a healthy addiction to the learning process. My mind was growing in its ability to process new information. My spirit was able to explore more options. I was starting to believe what I'd heard at all those AA meetings: *Keep coming back, it works!*

If I'd keep coming back to myself, checking in, and asking God for a little guidance, eventually I'd figure out who I was. Eventually I'd learn how to love myself. And maybe, just maybe, one day, I'd be like Sarah.

I'd know that I would be okay, too.

Chapter 5

Focus and Fear

I WAS 15, AND IT WAS A BIG DAY. The plans were all made. My mom and dad had to go to work, so Paw Paw, my Dad's dad, had agreed to take Best Smile Sarah and I to the DMV. That's right, we were ready to get our drivers' permits—a little piece of paper that would allow us to get behind the wheel and hit the open road.

We got there early, ready to take a test on the rules of the road. I passed the computer part easily and only had one last thing to accomplish before the permit would be mine. Step forward, put my head down, look in the little machine, and read off whatever line of numbers or letters were there in front of me.

There was only one problem. The letters and numbers were all fuzzy. I squinted and scrunched my face all sorts of ways, but what I thought I saw and then said out loud was not what was there.

"Miss, I'm sorry, but you failed the vision test. You'll have to come back and pass before you can get your permit."

I was heartbroken. How could a silly little thing like being able to see keep me from this big moment? I had for sure not seen that coming.

Corny one-liners aside, I was sad and disappointed, stewing as we made our way to school—Sarah with her permit and me empty-handed. But I was determined. Nothing was going to keep me from getting my drive on. Digging deep into my memory, I tried to remember where I'd left the glasses I'd stopped wearing years back.

I went home that day and dug to the back bottom of my closet, under clothes and shoes and who knows what else. And ta-da! There they were. They were bent and sat wonky and catty-corner on my face. But you know what? They did the trick. I begged my parents to take me back and later that afternoon I walked back up to that dang machine, passed that vision test, and got my permit.

It's funny to think back on the wave of emotions I rode that day. I went in thinking I was going to get my permit easily; I was confident (if not cocky) that I'd walk out with the right to drive. But dang it if the State required that I actually needed to be able to see what was in front of me (and see it clearly for that matter) before they'd allow me the right to hit the road. That requirement was for my safety and the safety of others.

I wish that same thing were true in other areas of life. Life would have been so much easier if there were other tests like that. Knowing myself, I would have chosen to take a test that would have measured if I was prepared to move forward and actively pursue my passions. Maybe it would've told me I wasn't quite ready a few months back when I tried to haul tail into transition. I would have failed. I would've had to pause and study up a bit first before I would've been permitted to proceed into my personal growth with caution.

A test like that would've been handy since I hadn't been able to see for myself that I'd become fuzzy on exactly who I was, what I stood for, and what I believed. But instead of being tested, I'd gotten behind the wheel and tried to drive blind, relying on myself and my naivety to guide me. And let's be honest, those hadn't gotten me too far in my new journey before I got lost.

My trip wasn't over though. I hadn't turned off the car or turned in my keys. I might not have reached my desired destination, but I was closer than where I'd started. I had learned plenty of lessons by mistake or chance. Either way, it was learning all the same. But I was ready to live and learn with more focus. I was craving a stronger sense of internal clarity—a clearer picture of where I wanted to head. And since I still hadn't found an easy test to help me figure that out, I had to find a way to do that for myself.

Already, I had decided I had to commit to self-reflection, conscious curiosity and intentionality in my decisions. Those were the routes I'd decided would help me grow and move forward in both my personal and professional life.

Intentional decision making meant that I was going to ask

myself questions about what I wanted and really consider my options, before deciding what I'd do about it—whatever "it" turned out to be at the time. I would try to focus on doing things on purpose for a purpose. The "for a purpose" part mattered to me; it meant that I had some destination in mind.

I was starting to form an idea of the quality of life that I wanted and knew was possible. And what's more, I was starting to believe that I deserved that life. No one had ever told me I didn't deserve the life of my dreams and I'd never thought it specifically. But, what I realized I'd done was look out into the world and see others living the life I thought I wanted and I envied them. I scrolled through perfect looking lives (even though I knew I was only getting the highlight reel) and wondered why mine couldn't be like that.

But some part of me was awakening to a few facts. I was in charge of my own life. I could create my very own highlight reel—one that included my personal and unique dreams. And I could do that because, well, because, why not? I was born into a country and into a time and place where I am free to chase whatever I want. I don't have to earn my chance to learn and do better for myself. The fact was, no one was holding me back from the life I had available to me but me.

Intentional living would require that I take time to be well informed and clear in my understanding of my options. Then I'd allow my gut and strategic mind to work together and reach a conclusion. That way, my decisions, even if not always "logical," at least were in line with what I thought would take me one step closer to the life of my dreams.

Intentional living sounded great, but I didn't know what it might actually look like for me. I had to try something to figure it out. So, one night as 2015 was nearing its end, I gave in to that need to slow down and get curious. I sat in the dark of my living room, staring at the beautiful, glowing lights of my Christmas tree. It was quiet, and calm, and hopeful.

Hanging high on the wall over the tree was a wide, red metal sign that read "Gather." It's like its arms were wide open, inviting me and reminding me why I was there.

Yes, this is the time to gather my thoughts.

I'd said I wanted clarity on what I wanted. I had even started seeking it. But now, this was the first time I'd given myself the space to actually try it. To gather my thoughts and write them down.

I got out a sheet of paper and drew lines to make three columns to have space for my personal, professional, and family goals. In the top left corner, I wrote down the top 5 things I really wanted for *myself*—things I wanted more of or to grow into. These were my hopes and dreams for the coming year:

- Self-awareness
- Speaker
- Leader
- Slower pace
- Stronger family and friend relationships

I didn't overthink what came to mind. I jotted them all down, and looking at them, they felt exactly right. Someone else's paper might have looked different; that was okay. This was a personal exercise. This was *my* paper and *my* life. And for the first time, I'd given myself the direction I so desperately wanted. But something was still missing.

Seconds later, in the middle of the page in all caps I wrote out the word, "*FEARLESS.*" Underneath that, right next to a heart, I wrote "*Growth!!!*"

I had been toying with an idea and finally decided to go with it in that moment. I would name the upcoming year for myself to give it meaning and purpose. No more resolutions that I'd ignore after a couple of weeks. My year needed a clear, intentional purpose. So, 2016 would be my year of Fearless Growth.

What did growth mean? How was I going to do that fearlessly? Breaking it down for myself, I focused on the individual words. The word growth meant forward movement to a higher place—one that I knew existed. And by fearless, I meant moving toward that higher place with bravery and courage, not shying away from things that seemed scary or daunting.

Fearless Growth.

It would be my mantra. I had written it down. I had taken it out of my brain and put it on paper. This was what I wanted, and I believed that God and the Universe would see my paper, hear my thoughts, and somehow give me plenty of opportunities to grow and achieve intentional living and fearless growing.

I couldn't forget a quote from Paulo Coelho's *The Alchemist*:

"And, when you want something, all the universe
conspires in helping you to achieve it."

I'd finished reading the book about the time I started on my Meant for More journey and wanted to believe that this line was true. I knew I wanted to grow fearlessly. What I didn't know is how God and the Universe would help me do it. But it didn't take long for little signs and gifts to show up along the road.

My first gift found its way to me in early 2016 as I was cleaning out the nightstand in my bedroom one weekend. As I threw away old papers, I came across a book by Louise Hay called *You Can Heal Your Life*. It was dusty, and there was a bookmark tucked inside about thirty pages in. I remembered exactly where this book came from—who had given it to me and why.

It was a sunny day in early spring 2008. It was crisp and clear outside without a cloud in the sky, but it was gray and dark in my world. My baby girl was lying in the middle of my mom's bed sleeping. She was close to eight weeks old. My son, who was a little over two at the time, was at the house as well, off playing in another room.

It was the middle of the day, and like so many others during my postpartum battle, it was a "bad" day for me. I was there with my mom and one of her lifelong best friends, Mary. I'd known Mary since I was a child. She was the director of the child care program I attended, and my mom had been one of her assistant directors.

We were all looking at my daughter. She was a tiny little ball, all curled up on the bed with the sun shining down on her.

Her little face pointed right at us, her eyes closed tight as she napped. The sun was streaming in through the bay window, filling the room with light. It was warm, but I could not control the cold dialogue in my mind.

I couldn't hold it in any more. Through hysterical sobs I cried out the soundtrack in my mind.

"There's nothing. I don't feel anything. I don't know what to do. I don't know what I'm doing. I can't do this. I don't know what to do with her. There's nothing."

Mary and my mom slowly swooped in to hold me—two women trying to protect me from myself. They whispered words of comfort, soothing, "You'll get through this," type things. It was a sad and severe moment of disconnection that fortunately ended within minutes but lingered in all of our hearts for years to come.

A few days after my meltdown, I received *You Can Heal Your Life* as a gift from Mary, and apparently, I'd opened it and read a few pages. But even though I'd stopped reading, for some reason, I'd kept it in my drawer. I must have known I'd need it someday. It was almost nine years since I first opened the book, but when I opened it this time, I saw something I hadn't remembered. Inside the front cover were these words: *Happy Healing, Dena! Jesus loves you, and so do I!*

I had to smile because I knew it was a beautiful gift. A gift I was meant to find and open again at this exact moment in my life. I started reading the book every day, and every single word was a mind-blowing experience.

I had never heard of Louise Hay, but she became a friend and mentor to me. She was over 90 years old, known for her self-help, motivational, and holistic teachings. She believed that individuals were responsible for their own experiences and that each person must learn to love themselves. She encouraged the use of positive affirmations and releasing resentments. And she taught that people created illness in their own bodies, putting their bodies at some "dis-ease" because of negative thought patterns they allowed themselves to feed into.

The concepts were new to me, but I was open, and receptive, and ready to try to learn. What could it hurt to layer on a new line of thinking? By widening the perspectives available to me, I was finding I had so many more options to deal with all the new information I was trying to absorb. And I wanted to add some of her tools to my growth toolkit.

On top of my newly created morning check-in and Serenity Prayer time in bed, I added reading from *You Can Heal Your Life* to my morning ritual. I also added reading from two different devotionals, both called *Jesus Calling*. They were written by the same exact author, Sarah Young, but one was the children's version and one was the adult version. I grabbed something different from reading both perspectives.

So, after I gathered whatever Divine guidance I could from my prayers and devotionals, I'd wrap up with a chapter or so from *You Can Heal Your Life*. My morning ritual got a bit longer, but it was worth the effort. Louise's book (yes, I'd decided we should be on a first name basis) layered in exercises and affirmations that were new to me, and I tried each one. I wanted to make them part of my new conscious, intentional way of living.

And that's where my love with Post-It notes began. I'd always liked those sticky little things, but in my quest for intentional growth, they became a mainstay in my life. I started writing Bible verses or Louise's recommended affirmations like, "*I love you,*" or, "*Accept you exactly as you are,*" on them. Then I'd post them up all around me in my office, my car, my bathroom, anywhere they'd stick.

In order to bring these new thoughts to the top of my mind, I had to look them in the eye over and over. I repeated them each time I saw them. I might have seemed a bit of a fool to some (my husband definitely thought I was nuts when I started writing on the bathroom mirrors with markers), but that's what growth looked like to me then. I had to start somewhere.

Something unexpected began to happen as I continued to add new information to my mind. As I tried to keep my heart open and receptive to focusing on myself, my body chimed in and wanted to be heard, too. But instead of buzzing with excitement or chilling with calm, my body had other things in mind. My Meant for More journey would now come to include not only an emotional and intellectual journey, but a physical one as well.

I started waking up most mornings and quickly finding in my check-in that my body was not feeling great. In fact, it felt far from great. I was almost always nauseous, tummy rolling and skin prickling with nerves. One morning when I woke up to another morning check-in where I felt like crap, I decided to sit down and do an inventory of all the things my body was feeling—all the ailments I was working through.

In *You Can Heal Your Life*, there was a chapter called "The List." In it, there was a pretty simple chart to maneuver. It started with the Problem list over on the left, followed by the Probable Cause list in the middle, and then a New Thought Pattern on the far right. The Problem was the body ailment or area that was causing you grief. The Probable Cause was the situation or thought pattern that was most likely bringing the body to a pain point. And Louise's recommendation was to try to change the story by using an affirmation that was included in the New Thought Pattern.

Sign. Me. Up. I was totally game to try.

I sat there that morning and looked up all the areas in my body that were Problem areas—my stomach, bowels, abdominal cramps, anxiety, gas pains. Yeah, it was good times up in my body.

I wrote down all the Probable Causes associated with all the Problems my body had. Not surprisingly, a pattern quickly presented itself.

Fear of the new. Inability to assimilate to the new.
Fear. Undigested ideas.
Fear of deadlines. Anger of past. Afraid to let go.
Fear. Stopping the process.
Fear of letting go of the old. Not trusting the flow and process of life.

The list confirmed that what I was experiencing physically was in line with my emotional state. I was scared sh*tless. When I saw "fear" repeatedly on that piece of paper, it all seemed to make sense. I was terrified. I was scared of living through the new growth that I had asked for. I was afraid to let go and actually move forward because I didn't know what was coming next for me, my career, or my marriage.

I had to laugh. Here I was in my self-proclaimed year of Fearless Growth, where I imagined I'd be standing tall, and proud, and strong, beating my freaking chest growing in leaps in bounds. But instead, I realized that I was terrified to experience the things I'd asked for. Fearless, it turns out, I was not.

But I had a choice.

And that year, I chose not to give in to fear. Instead I chose to let Louise guide me. I chose to give some new thought patterns a try. And when I wrote them down, they almost instantly made me feel better.

I trust the process of life.
I digest life with ease.
I love and approve of myself and trust the process of life.
I am safe.
I relax and let life flow through me.

I had some complicated personal baggage to sort through no doubt. But this was a start. And the affirmation that hit me the most—the one I wrote down on Post-It notes and repeated in my mind—was simple:

I am safe.

Insert a deep breath.

I. Am. Safe.

God, it felt great to say, even if I didn't feel it right there at the moment. I believed it, and one day, maybe I'd feel it, too.

That morning inventory was eye-opening. It made me even more curious about my fears in general. And since I was telling myself that I was safe, I decided that I could intentionally try and dig into my top fears. During Discovery Day, I narrowed down my top three fears: falling, death, and loss of control. So, I thought on each one to see what I could learn about myself in the process.

First on the list was falling. And as far as I'm concerned, falling stinks. If a fall didn't hurt (which it normally did), it was for sure always totally embarrassing if other people saw it happen. A pretty basic fear, right? Not much else to learn about falling. I didn't go out and try to take any tumbles. And I didn't go searching for heights that might lead to plummets. I learned that for me, it's fine to be scared of falling. It made sense.

I also didn't have to think too hard on death. Death—my death, the death of others, death in general—had always made my tummy nervous. And again, it made sense. Death is one of the only things we can't talk to someone about who has experienced it. It is one of the only true unknowns *and* true certainties in life.

But over coffee one day, a former colleague of mine mentioned she had read a book about death as part of a course she was taking on grief counseling. I was in "let's learn and grow mode," so I did what seemed like the right thing to do. I asked her and another friend to reread the book with me. We could meet up and have a little Death Book Club. It was a weird request, but I had weird friends who agreed.

So, we read *Staring at the Sun—Overcoming the Terror of Death* by Irvin Yalom. And as one does in a Death Book Club, we got together and talked it out over Thai food. (Because comfort food digesting while talking about the fact that you won't exist forever made total sense!)

After reading the book and hashing it out with the ladies, I realized that it wasn't necessarily "death" I was scared of; I was scared of dying with unfulfilled dreams. The thought of dying with life unlived scared me and made me sad.

What if I never get to speak in front of people about things that matter to me?

It was a revelation. A revelation that left me torn, since again I had a fear of living through the experience of a professional transition and a fear of leaving things unlived. How could I move forward when I had some sort of mental and emotional emergency brake permanently in the on position leaving me stranded? It was a question I'd have to keep circling.

But I was still curious about the last of my top 3 fears: the loss of control. I had some personal insights into falling and death, but the loss of control was harder for me to describe. As I thought on it, I asked myself questions to try and figure it out.

If I'm not in control, then what happens?

After a quick pause, the internal response took me back.

If you lose control, you could die.

Whoa! It was my 9-year-old self remembering that lesson. I had learned from Louise to love and respect the inner child she believed we all carried with us into adulthood, so I listened to what the little girl in me had to say. But as an adult, I wanted to dig a bit more into the actual words she was saying. I wanted to understand.

I went to the online thesaurus and looked up "control," curious to find synonyms and antonyms. Nerdy? Sure. A little weird? Maybe, but fun to me. There were lots of great, seemingly positive synonyms—words like authority, discipline, guidance, management, and direction. Those all sounded good.

But what about the opposite meanings? Since I had a fear of the *loss of* control, what was the opposite? What's the opposite of control? Words like chaos, neglect, weakness, helplessness. And then, the kicker: *freedom.*

Oh, sweet Jesus, there it was. *I was scared of freedom.*

Losing control and feeling weak, chaotic, or helpless, well, those made sense to be scared of. Why would anyone want those things? But the realization that I might actually have a fear of freedom—of living in a state of being free and able to do some-thing at will—*that* threw me for a loop. I like to believe that God giggled when I found that little gift.

I was too scared to take hold of the free will that I and every other living human had access to. Or was I? I didn't hear an outright challenge from God or the Universe, but if I had, I think this is how it would have gone down:

> *God: You said you wanted to have Fearless Growth, Dena. Well, you've got a ton of fear in there that does not want you to change things up. It does not want you to grow. So, what do you choose?*

> *Me: Oh, hey there, God. I choose to believe that my brain will believe what I tell it, and you've got my back on this, right?*

I thought God would have said "Yes!" So, I tried something new. I tried to refocus my mind. Years back I'd failed to get that license to drive because my eyes couldn't translate to my brain what they saw. And now, even though I didn't need glasses to see what was in front of me, I still needed something to help me stay conscious and intentional in my growth, even when it was scary.

It was worth a try to see if I could use words in a whole new way—as affirmations that might help bring clarity to my life. I would have to hold tight to the belief that one day, all would be well. So, I told that brain of mine this simple line for what felt like 1 million times a day.

> *I am safe.*
> *I am safe.*
> *I. Am. Safe.*

I wrote, spoke, and whispered those words as I continued to have conversations with myself, my husband, and some of my closest friends and coworkers about what my next professional steps should be. Then finally one day, I had a conversation with the managing partner of our firm. I told him over drinks that I wasn't going to be with the firm for the long haul. I didn't know what that meant exactly, but I had to keep figuring out how to make my professional dreams a reality, and to do that, odds were I would have to walk away.

He listened as I rambled on. When I finally stopped talking, he had a chance to speak.

"Dena. Everything is going to be okay. Want to know how I know?"

I nodded and waited with curious anticipation.

"Because you are smiling."

I was smiling. I had done it. I had trusted myself and the process of life. I still couldn't see exactly where I was headed, but I'd been brave enough to control what I could control: myself and my choices. I hadn't gotten rid of my fears, but I'd decided I could and would grow in spite of them.

Fearless growth meant that I'd get to know my fears better and on purpose. Then I'd ask my fears to get in the car with me as we continued to move forward. We—me and my fears—we could be safe. We could grow together. Shoot, I even had a roadmap. So what if it was only a piece of paper with a pencil drawn sketch for the year to come?

It wasn't fancy, but it was something new.

And it was working.

Chapter 6

All the Feels

ONE MORNING IN EARLY SUMMER OF 2016, I woke up into the pitch black. It was way too early to get up, but there was no way I'd be going back to sleep. I tried my morning check-in but could already feel the anxiety creeping in as I lay with my eyes closed. My body was jittery, and my mind was racing.

About what though? I couldn't name one specific thing. I was stuck in limbo and the unknowns of each day combined with the unknowns of the future were freaking me out. So, I laid there, but before I could even make it to the Serenity Prayer, I got up and tried to sneak out without waking up JP.

What is going on with you, Dena? Why are you freaking out?

I paced through the kitchen and living room before deciding to go out to our pool house. I didn't want to disturb my family. I also hoped to remove myself from my internal line of questioning. But alone in the back room of a separate structure away from my sleeping family, I still wasn't alone.

Turns out, I couldn't distance myself from myself. I paced, trying anything to shake the feelings, fear, nervousness, and maybe even a little dread. I screamed in a pillow, punched it a few times, and tried to cry. But nothing seemed to make the unpleasant feelings stop. My nerves were speeding out of control.

After an intense hour, I pulled myself together enough to make it through the morning routine. I got the kids and myself ready to go and out of the house. But once at the office, I still couldn't get myself together. I was a ticking time bomb, no idea what would be the thing to finally make me blow. I brought in my nearest and dearest friends at work and rambled on about my emotional state.

I joked that it would be awesome to have half a Xanax to get me through. I wasn't taking any prescription drugs, but I had during my postpartum days. They had been a God-send for me then. But after both kiddos, once I'd been emotionally ready, I gradually eased off the pills and hadn't felt that I needed them since.

But I remembered the slow seep of calm that followed that magic pill. And the thought of easing my internal chaos sounded wonderful. I joked again that I wouldn't mind taking one. Then, one of my friends offered me one of theirs.

And, I might have accepted the gracious offer. Well, not might have. I did. I accepted it wholeheartedly. I took the pill, a whole one when I probably should have only taken half. I'm generally not one to take other's prescription drugs, but I was desperate to chill out. I sat at my desk and savored the slow spread of ease that I was hoping for.

It felt good not to feel so much in the moment, but later that night, I was disappointed in myself. Not disappointed that I took the pill. It has a very specific and necessary purpose for so many people. It was something I myself have needed and taken before. But this time was different. I wasn't battling prolonged anxiety or depression. I was battling my current fear of the unknown. And I was disappointed that I had tried to run from the experiences that I said I wanted.

Months back in January, I'd included self-awareness as one of my top 5 wants on my Fearless Growth sheet. Little did I realize that self-awareness would consist of me having to you know, be self-aware! A quick Google search reminded me that self-awareness was a conscious knowledge of one's own character, feelings, motives, and desires.

I had already had chances to think about my true character and motives. I had a good idea of my passions and dreams. But the feelings part? That was going to take deliberate effort. And instead of putting in that effort, I had chosen to pop that pill and numb my feelings. I'd been numb before, and it had done me no good.

After my soul awakening, I realized that, for so many years, I was nearly numb emotionally. I laughed, but not too much. And when I did, it either felt forced or shallow. I didn't get angry too often. I wasn't a fighter. I couldn't even think of the last time JP and I had fought. I avoided any type of potential conflict like the plague, at work or at home.

For many years, I wasn't interested in dealing with anything where emotions ran hot or heavy. I also wasn't a big fan of feeling sad. I hadn't cried much, and when I did, I nipped it in the bud before the tears could even roll down my cheeks.

I dodged complicated or negative emotions like you'd dodge nasty potholes. If I touched on something raw or painful, my cheeks might get red and I might even tear up, but then . . . wooosh! I'd dart around to some other thing or throw out some positive one-liner to try and avoid falling in and getting bumped and bruised.

Jules told me that out of all her years in practice with all her clients, I was one of the best at quickly diverting myself away from the hard feelings. That's right, I'm a winner! Where was my trophy? When she told me this during my first baby steps of self-awareness, I recognized the pattern in myself immediately, but I didn't know if I could try what she was asking of me. She wanted me to put my feeling dodger award aside and actually try to sit in my feelings longer than a second.

That was a tough challenge. Sit in sadness, anger, loneliness, and fear? *Really, Jules?* I didn't know if I could handle the sharp curves of all I was feeling. Would I be able to stay in some sort of control? Or would I ride those curves up on two wheels always at risk of rolling over?

As I was trying to live and grow fearlessly, my emotions kept flaring up more and more, and at some point, I realized that if I was really going to develop into a stronger version of myself, my growth was going to have to include my emotional strength and stamina. I would never have thought it would be such a huge part of my journey, but it was turning out to be.

I was going to have to try and figure out what to do with all these feelings—many of which were foreign to me. I'd spent a lifetime squashing them down or avoiding them altogether. But honestly, those patterns of behavior hadn't served me well. And I wasn't going to keep asking my friends for pills to pop. I was ready to try a new thought pattern from Louise.

It is safe for me to express my emotions. I am willing to feel.

It was time to try something new . . . again.

On top of therapy sessions with Jules and vent sessions with girlfriends, I kept layering in more intentional reading. I was curious how I could live with all the feelings I was having when lo and behold, another gift fell in my lap. Alisa gifted me Holley Gerth's book *You're Already Amazing—Embracing Who You Are, Becoming All God Created You to Be.* I underlined almost every other sentence in her book, folded down pages throughout, and had notes jotted in the margins.

But one chapter stole the show. It was chapter 4, entitled "Why Do I Feel This Way?" And it had my name written all over it. The premise of the chapter was that by holding emotions too much in check, you cut yourself short on the full experience life has to offer. Seemed straight-forward, but it was mind-blowing to me.

There were exercises to do to help you think back on how you processed emotions all the way from childhood. There was an entire page with a list of different feelings—EIGHTY of them! If you'd have asked me that before the book, I probably would only have been able to think of three emotions. Maybe just happy, sad, and mad. On the pages that followed the crazy long list of emotions, another exercise had you circle ones that were "NOT okay to feel . . .," ones that "I allow myself to feel . . .," and finally, ones that "I don't allow myself to feel."

It was fascinating. Each exercise was eye-opening for me. My self-awareness was in high gear. I couldn't stop myself from writing notes in the margins.

My emotional pattern is to push down and not share to protect myself.

But I also jotted down that I wanted to be more accepting of feeling, sharing, and learning how to balance conflicting feelings. And then I was struck by her next nugget of wisdom: "God's intent is for us to appropriately experience the full range of emotions . . . When we limit our negative emotions, we limit our capacity to experience positive ones, too."

I stared at the picture she included of a line representing a full range of emotions—all the way from negative on one end to positive on the other. There was a neutral spot in the middle, and she explained that as I put a barrier on how far I'd go down the negative side of the line, my heart would put an equal-distanced marker over on the positive side. By limiting my maximum sadness, I was limiting my max happiness, too.

As I read, questions swirled in my brain.

Wait one second. I've been limiting myself? By not wanting to feel some of the "harder" emotions in my life and avoiding them, I've been keeping myself from the ones I desperately want to experience? I've narrowed the emotional experience of my life, but I can change that? I can choose to feel more?

My heart smiled and answered my brain's questions.

Heart: Yes, yes, and yes.

But my brain kept pushing.

*Brain: Okay, Heart, so, if I go ahead and continue to feel
and allow you to explore more of these not so pleasant
things, you might start feeling more of that joy you
are wanting so badly?*

Heart: Yup, Holley said so!

Brain: Prove it.

That's what came to mind. *Prove this works!*

Yet again, logic needed something to hold on to and a proven process to follow. And it didn't take me long to connect a few dots on how I could prove this new idea. It came from none other than my favorite morning talk show, The Bobby Bones Show.

Some may not know Bobby Bones, but for over 15 years, I commuted into town and listened to the show during my average 45-minute ride. I had time to fill, and I filled it with the voices of Bobby, Amy, Lunchbox, Eddie, Ray, and several others who had come and gone over the years. They became part of my morning routine. They started to feel like my friends.

For me, they were easy to love! On top of their focus on

positivity and campaigns like Pimpin' Joy, a beautiful memorial movement following Amy's mom and the inspiring way she battled cancer, Bobby was also passionate about hard work. When he started sharing his mantra—*Fight. Grind. Repeat.*—attached to his second book, *Fail Until You Don't*, I was knee deep into trying to expand my emotional spectrum.

Fight. Grind. Repeat.

For whatever reason, that resonated with me, at least partially. There seemed to be something more than effort infused into Bobby's mantra. It felt angry to me. When I would wear the branded shirt or hear Bobby talk about it, it felt like I was gritting my teeth and trying to go after something, but I couldn't quite get completely behind the words. The phrase felt more daunting to me than inspiring.

But for where I was in my life, trying to dig in and feel all the stinking feels, there was some part of his *Fight. Grind. Repeat.* loop that was leading me to a whole other loop altogether. Then it came to me. My own mantra: *Feel. Deal. Heal.*

I repeated those three words as I willed myself to feel more. I started saying them when I would sit on Jules' couch and try to stay in the hard feelings longer (which was really hard work). As I sat in the feelings longer, I had to start actually dealing with the emotional and physical responses that were unpleasant. It was wildly uncomfortable.

And when the feelings got tough, I wanted to get going. That had always been my natural instinct. I wanted to do some of my award-winning dodging and avoiding, but then I'd pause, regroup, and repeat my mantra: *Feel. Deal. Heal.*

It seemed that every day I was faced with an opportunity to feel something, and then I'd have a chance to deal with it. Another day, another choice. So. Many. Choices. And dealing with it looked different every time. One time it might have been to take time to breathe. Another it might have been to say out loud what I was feeling—to put a voice to the emotional response. Whatever it was, I was committed to the process of expanding my emotional range.

Feel. Deal. Heal. You can do it, Dena.

I journaled about the fight I was grinding through with all these feelings.

Some of the feelings that have found their way to me lately include fear, jealousy, anger, resentment, discontent, and loneliness—feelings that seem to be forbidden to talk about let alone feel. I need to go ahead and feel them though, even if it means my body temperature rises, my stomach turns, and my brain reels. Until.

Until when? How do I know when it's time to move along from these feelings? It isn't fun. It's quite uncomfortable actually and physically draining. How long do I have to sit in them?

Tonight, I'll just focus on feeling them and worry about the resolution another day.

Even with all the emotional expansion and all the feeling and dealing that came with it, I was grappling with exactly how I'd even know that I was healed—healed from childhood wounds, relationship scars, and old patterns of thought and behavior. I had no clue if I was healing. But I knew I was making progress. I was changing my emotional ways. Getting through two legs of my *Feel. Deal. Heal.* process was a huge win for me.

Admitting to myself and others that it was difficult to sit in hard to process emotions was one thing. But then consciously choosing to sit in them? Well, that was a gold star for me! A star I was proud to have earned. The scary side of those forbidden feelings was losing some of their power, and I was starting to feel like a winner.

And the prize I got was priceless.

One night as we were tucking the kids into bed and doing our nighttime ritual of sharing three things we were grateful for plus a bonus "Tell Me Something Good" where we sang the tune just like on the Bobby Bones Show, someone said something that was funny.

And I laughed.

Not a half-hearted, fake giggle. No, it was a laugh from down deep in my belly. I almost didn't recognize the sound as my own, but it was me! The sound of my joy-filled laughter felt foreign and at the same time, so natural that I nearly burst into tears of joy.

After that first outburst, I started to feel more and more feels. Sometimes I felt them all in the same day. Tears started to flow more naturally, from joy and sadness. My laughter rolled out more easily. And I even welcomed the heat of anger and frustration to take their turn, too. I had expanded my emotional range! All of those feels had their space now, giving my life the color and vibrancy that I longed to experience in my life.

Heart: Take that, Brain. How's that for proof?

Brain: I'll think about it.

All I could think about now was how thankful I was. I was thankful for the struggles and the emotions that wrecked me and built me back up. I was thankful for all the people in my life who were spurring me on—people that I paid to counsel me, people who wrote life-changing books I could read, and people that only spoke to me through my car speakers. I was full of gratitude. I was even thankful for myself and how far I'd already come.

When I thought back to where I'd started and all the small moments that had led me to where I was now, I hadn't consciously thought of all that I'd mapped out when I dreamed up the Meant for More way. Yet sure enough, I was changing with each step.

Each slight adjustment (or sometimes 180-degree turn!) from my old ways of thinking and being to my new ones were course corrections guiding me along my path. It was my very own journey of self-discovery. A journey that included lots of feeling, dealing, and maybe one-day, healing.

I was thankful to be alive. I knew that there were still bumps and bruises ahead of me, but I had joy and hope riding in the car with me. They were keeping me company, so I knew I'd end up somewhere safe someday, with the sun shining down on me and a big old smile on my face. I was becoming my very own proof of concept that I was in fact Meant for More—destined to have the life of my dreams.

Chapter 7

Poolside Epiphany

"HOPE DEFERRED MAKES THE HEART SICK, but a longing fulfilled is a tree of life."

Proverbs 13:12 jumped off the page during my morning devotional time with Louise and Jesus. I'd done the hard work to get myself out of autopilot mode and finally felt like I had both hands firmly on the steering wheel, but I still didn't know the next stop on my journey. As I kept opening up my Bible, the verses there were becoming guides all on their own.

This verse in Proverbs was exactly that. I had given up hope before. I knew what a sick heart felt like, and I didn't want to go back that way again. I had to chase the longing. I had to choose to believe that my dreams were in my heart and soul for a reason. I had to keep choosing hope. I had to keep seeking and finding my way toward the tree of life—my tree of life. The life where

I was healthy, rooted, and able to spread my arms out wide and dance in the wind.

But did I genuinely want the life of my dreams? I said I did. I told myself as much, and now I'd told others, too. My husband, my family and friends, and even my boss, for goodness sakes! But I needed more action to support all the words I was saying. They were great words of hope, but words alone weren't going to get me anywhere. That was until I found that string of words in Proverbs that would become my guiding North Star.

I let it guide me first to another moment of self-awareness. I was beginning to be more honest with myself about how lonely I had become. It had been painful to feel completely alone inside of a marriage, and even though JP and I were actively working to make things better, I was realizing that he alone couldn't meet all my needs for connection.

Since early on my pattern had been to attach to a boy since such a young age, I had never invested heavily in relationships with other girls, now turned women. JP became my best friend our sophomore year in high school, and from then on, female relationships took a back seat.

But I had written on my Fearless Growth sheet that I wanted stronger friend relationships. That was the longing. And there was no reason to wait. Now was as good a time as any to figure out how to make those relationships stronger. It was time for a girls' trip. I just had to hope that my best friend would love what I had in mind.

"Alisa, I need a getaway. You game?"

We needed some girl time away from our families (which

together was two husbands and six children). She was all in! We found a women's event called the Belong Tour in Dallas, an easy spot for us to meet since it was about the same distance for us both to travel. We bought tickets, made hotel reservations, and counted down the days for our getaway adventure.

I was the first to get there on a ridiculously beautiful day near the end of September 2016. Driving by myself for almost four hours had been a treat, allowing me to listen to any music, or podcast, or e-book I wanted without interruption. When I showed up at the W Hotel, I immediately shot Alisa a text.

"I'm here. We fancy."

I checked in, found our room, and decided to head straight to the pool, computer, book, and Diet Coke in hand.

God, it was beautiful. The rooftop pool looked out and into blue skies. It wasn't too crowded and wasn't too hot. I leaned back and took a few deep, relaxing breaths. And that's when it hit me.

This is the LIFE!

This. Is. The. Life.

I grabbed my computer and started typing.

I'll be honest. At this very moment, I am sitting in a lounge chair by a pool in the middle of the day. Sitting. Relaxing. Unwinding. Breath by deep breath. I'm dreamy. I'm hopeful.

I'm thinking over and over that this is the life. I know this can't be everyday life, but sweet, precious Jesus, it is my life today, and I'm enjoying it right now in this moment. The breeze is soft and cool. I can hear water running, and luckily, it's not making me feel like I have to pee. There is not a cloud in the beautiful blue sky in front of me. This is my life right now, and I'm thankful for it.

But what is LIFE?

In Holley Gerth's book, *You're Already Amazing*, she said that LIFE equals "Love Is Faith Expressed." It is how you share your love with the world. It is your life's mission. Your calling. Your why. Your only you can do it exactly that way because you were born exactly that way to do exactly that thing. I loved every page of her book and have been dreaming of creating my own personal LIFE statement, which in this moment has finally become clear to me.

My name is and will continue to be Dena Jansen. I was born August 11th, 1979. I entered my own journey that day, and here I sit, over 37 years later, and I'm finally brave enough to type out these words about what the heck I'm here on this planet to do.

My LIFE statement is this: *To breathe light and life into potential seeking people and companies.*

By working with these potential seekers, I will gain energy, faith, love, strength, wisdom, and courage from being part of their something bigger.

I love words. So, I will speak. I love to communicate. So, I will write, type, talk, and connect to people with intentional messages. I want to inspire and be inspired. So, I will work with people and companies that inspire me so that we are on equal footing and have the capacity to give and receive.

I am here to share, shout, or whisper words of bravery and hope to people desperately seeking themselves and their dreams. These are people that have proven that they are ready, willing, and able to put in hard work to grow and seek their personal potential, which is ever just out of their reach. This will be my happy place.

This LIFE statement will guide me. It will be at the core of all my decisions. If I hold true to this, I know wonderful things will happen. Things that I can dream of now and also have zero ability to fathom. I have faith and hope in my potential and can't wait to see what each new day holds.

I'd never been so clear before. Never had the words fallen out like that. Maybe the peace of the moment allowed it to bubble up. I didn't know and didn't care. I just knew it felt amazing, freeing. I read it and re-read it at least a hundred times. And it made me so stinking happy.

For the first time I'd been able to explain the higher level vision and mission for my life that I believed God had planted in my heart and soul. I had zoomed out from all the blurry details I kept getting lost in and could see a clearer picture of my ultimate destination. *Whoa.*

My girls' weekend only got better. Alisa and I spent that night and following day surrounded by thousands of other women of faith listening to several strong-willed women speaking, singing, playing beautiful music, making us do squats in the stands (somehow even those made me and Alisa cry), sharing words of hope, inspiration, telling us our stories mattered, our dreams mattered, and most importantly, that we all belonged.

I'd grown up during middle school and high school active in the church and found that I was experiencing what I used to call the "church camp high." For me, that was the week or so after having been submersed in Bible studies and praise and worship music where you were still on fire for Jesus. As we walked out at the end of the event feeling strong and hopeful, I didn't want to come down from the high yet. I wasn't ready to head home and back to reality. I wanted to sit in these powerful feelings longer.

So, I did something I normally would never have done. I decided to be spontaneous and stay another night. Might seem tame for some, but it was wild for me. I had to prod Alisa into it, but once we got the husbands and kiddos squared away, we enjoyed one more night away. A few more hours of time to connect, talk, and dream, at the pool and later over chips and queso. One more night to go to bed feeling full of friendship and new memories.

It was back to reality the next day, and we went our separate ways—back to our homes and our families. But as I was rolling down the highway, I couldn't get my mind to stop rolling along with me. I was driving home to Buda, the same hometown and same city that well-known faith-based author and speaker, Jen Hatmaker, also called home. Jen was fresh on my mind as she'd been one of the speakers at the event that weekend.

I had crossed paths with her on a few occasions at a movie theater or at the local yoga studio in our small town, but we weren't buds. I shared her passion for words, and I for sure had a longing for a professional career somewhat similar to her own. I didn't feel called to be a preacher. Me and Jesus were clear on that. But watching her and the other women up on the stage lit a fire in my belly.

My church camp high was apparently still riding shotgun because shortly after pulling into my driveway, I decided I needed to unpack my car and then unpack my hopes and dreams into a letter to the one and only Jen Hatmaker.

Why not? We lived in the same city. Maybe we could be friends. The internal debate began.

Does this make any sense? NO.
Will she ever read it? MAYBE NOT.
Am I going to do it anyways? YUP.

I got out paper and a pen and dove right in.

October 2, 2016

Jen,

May I call you Jen? As if we are already friends. I mean, we have actually met, and sat at the same table, and had a meal, and then watched Twilight together. I'm pretty sure homemade shirts were involved, so let's assume that makes us at least two humans that can have fun and be friendly.

Here's the deal: I'm a lane changer. Like blinker on, looking to both sides for real life lane changer.

I have grown in ways that were unimaginable to me over the last year and a half, and my life is on the road again, but this time, I know where I am headed. Not like I know the actual address or what the name plate will say on the door when I get there (because those things are completely unknown), but I know my purpose—my sweet, precious calling that God placed in my heart.

About three hours before walking into the doors of the event, I wrote my LIFE statement. I have included it with this letter. Then for a day and a half, I listened to women of faith speak and share their truths. And guess what? They were so beautifully aligned. I have so many stories that I want to share. So many words, dreams, and fears that I want to share with you because I feel charged to do so. I am a firm believer that it will happen in God's time.

So, this is my invitation to you, and this seems like the absolute most fun way to do this.

Are you in a place where you would like to hear more?

____ Yes, open ears.
____ No, I'm not quite ready but interested.
____ Never, continue to pray for clearer signs.

I have included a self-addressed stamped envelope and will wait to see where you might be. If it never comes, well, God will see me through my disappointment. I will have been brave in following what my voice was telling me to do.

If you choose to say yes to this, you too are brave and fun. And you aren't signing up for a long-term commitment or a coffee. I don't even drink coffee. You are signing up for a pen pal. I just want to share some fun things, what ifs, and precious parts of me that I feel God is ready for me to share. So that's it.

I can only imagine this is one of the weirdest letters you might have gotten, and it's the strangest one I've written. But it was time. It was time for me to attempt connection with you. I do that with calm, and peace, and knowledge that my desire might not be met in the same way from you, but dang it, I can't control the outcome. I can only take the first step.

Thank you for considering this!
Dena Jansen
Proverbs 13:12

I did it. I wrote the letter. The envelope was thick and required extra postage since I included my LIFE statement and a self-addressed stamped return envelope. I packaged it up, put it in the mailbox, and put the red flag up. Alisa and I laughed hard talking about it over the phone. JP let me know he thought I was crazy. But I was hopeful.

I checked the mailbox for a few weeks with mild anticipation. Ultimately, I never heard back from Jen, and I probably won't ever. But sending that letter had absolutely been worth it. It felt so good to play, to be brave, and to share myself with absolutely no guarantee of the outcome. It was fun to take a risk, be a little wild, and do something that was completely illogical.

It was the first thing I did that was in alignment with my LIFE statement. I had attempted to connect to another potential seeking person with an intentional message. Sure, it might have been a little overkill for my first shot, but what could I say? I was a Fearless Grower. I had also chosen to not defer my hope. I went for what I felt compelled to do, and it made me feel alive. There was truth in that ancient proverb.

What I didn't realize though was that in my silly attempt to connect to Jen, I was really starting to connect to myself. I was a potential seeker with a vision for my life that would no longer settle for status quo.

I was finally starting to get my own message.

Chapter 8

Let Go and Let Life

"CRY, DENA. JUST CRY."

I was a young teenager when Michelle, my youth pastor and surrogate second mother said those words to me. She whispered them to me like a soft, yet stern command. She'd have me all wrapped up in her big old hug repeating those directions.

"Cry, Dena. Just cry."

And every time, my tears would finally fall, giving into her words and her tight grip of love.

I might have been a natural born leader and speaker, but I was not a natural crier. Growing up, stress and hormones would build up, leaving me feeling full and jittery. And since I had taken to self-protective stuffing and didn't yet understand how to expand my emotional range, it had always taken some prompting to get me to let it out. Somehow, Michelle had always been able to create the space for me to let out what I had shoved way down deep.

Now all these years later and only a matter of weeks since my illustrious girls' weekend and church camp high, I wasn't on a high anymore. In fact, I was low—gut-wrenchingly low. I had come so far in figuring out myself, my career, my marriage, and my friends, but my emotional dam was stuck again. I could tell that I needed a good old teary breakdown, but I couldn't figure out how to get my tears to fall. Where was Michelle when I needed her?

This time it wasn't adolescent stress and hormones that had my emotions in overdrive. In the last few months, I'd been thrown a more adult size dose of stress. At work, I found out that I needed to take over a ton of work that I hadn't expected. I was capable, but it meant that I had to forget about any movement on speaking or sharing my LIFE statement. I had to put my head down and audit my little heart out.

I started to believe what I'd read in a few books. As people began seeking their true selves and evolving into new versions of themselves, seemingly bad things would show up and get in the way. In Jen Sincero's book, *You are a Badass,* she called it the "Big Snooze." She said, "The Big Snooze will do everything it can to stop you from changing and growing."

And BS, as she called it, might throw in emotional blocks or even get physical to try and make you stop growing into unknown territory. I'd experienced both physical and emotional blocks before. The body ailment inventory I'd done months back had already shown me all the ways BS would try and revolt against my growth and keep me living in fear.

I'd worked through it then, with all the "I am safe" affirmations I could whisper or shout. I'd even spread my emotional wings, dug into harder emotions, and been gifted with laughter. But it seemed as much as I felt the need to get misty-eyed, another emotional block had wedged itself into my tear ducts. And I couldn't figure it out. Why couldn't I cry?

Cry, Dena! Just cry.

I chalked it up to the work stress. I ticked off my work to-do list slowly but surely. I was going to weather this storm with as much grace as I could muster. But then BS busted into my life again. And this time, it came to play for real.

It was a Sunday night. JP and I were home and the kids were already in bed when my mom came by the house. She dropped her keys on the counter and started into a quick mix of darting dialogue. I was trying to keep up when I thought I heard her allude to the fact that she wanted to divorce my dad.

I looked right at my husband and quietly mouthed, "Did you just hear what I thought I just heard?"

He nodded back in reply.

I don't know whose eyes were wilder: mine, my husband's, or my mom's. Crazy things were happening. Okay, maybe it wasn't crazy. It wasn't even the first time they'd separated. The last time was while I was in high school, but they reunited after a few months. My parents' marriage had seen its own highs and lows. It wasn't something we—my mom, dad, me, or my sister—talked about. But we'd all experienced their struggles. So, my mom's decision wasn't a complete shock, but it still threw me into codependency mode, worrying about both of my parents.

Wheels of distraction from my own journey were in motion, and I imagine the Big Snooze was loving it. The added work stress had been a light tap compared to my parents' marriage dissolving, a much more personal blow. It was an emotional nail that blew my tire wide open and let loose all the feelings I had built up over the recent months. Anger, sadness, stress, fear, frustration, concern—I felt it all within moments. But over the days and weeks that followed, I did what I did best: I kept all my feelings buckled in tight.

I tried to patch myself and my emotions together. Of course, what was happening with my parents was on my mind but familiar patterns of pushing the actual feeling and dealing to the bottom of my to-do list felt easier than the alternative. I certainly didn't want to sit in the complicated mess of feelings. But one night just a couple weeks later, as JP and I were getting ready to head to a concert with near and dear friends, I got the text.

"I told your dad. I'm not at the house, but I'll check on him later."

The reality was setting in. And just like that, my hazard lights went to blinking. But as our friends arrived, I went right back to stuffing.

"Hey! Almost ready! Oh yeah, one thing though, my mom just told my dad she wants a divorce. Cool."

I tried to walk away and distance myself from feeling the sadness and childhood-turned-buried-adult fears that were starting to bubble up. I tried to physically flee the space. As I started to walk away though, my friend Cassie had other plans. She walked right up to me, uninvited, and wrapped her arms around me.

How did she know? Had she talked to Michelle?

As I tried the quick squeeze and release method, she squeezed me tighter, down low and around my back. She wouldn't let go. I didn't fight; I didn't have the energy. Then, the floodgates opened and the sobs that had been building started to fall out, right there in the middle of my living room in front of her husband and mine.

Looking back now, I am sure that those tears had been there since I was 9 years old, the night Dad didn't come home. I'd never let them out, but here they were now, finding their way to the floor. The child that lived within the adult I'd become was sad and scared for her dad who had just received a big blow. The little girl within me worried that the man he was today might feel out of control. The adult me jumped to the unspoken fear that we shared—my mom, my sister and me. The fear that he would instantly go to drinking again.

Those that loved my dad dearly had similar concerns, and we all made sure he was safe that night. He did go MIA for a bit, giving us all a scare. But we later found out that again, like so many years before, he'd taken to driving miles and miles in his truck to try and clear his mind.

And honestly, I found I needed the same thing. I needed to clear my mind. My way of getting my head straight was to write another letter. I'd tried it with my "friend" Jen and didn't know if it ever even made it, but this letter was different. It was different because I filled it with personal pleas for my dad to make healthy choices, to know that I loved him and believed that he could weather this crappy personal storm. And I knew this letter would make it because I hand delivered it to him days later.

I had the letter in hand as I knocked on the front door. The same front door that I had gone through almost one year before when my marriage was falling apart. Somehow the letter didn't fall as he opened the door and reached out, sobbing into my arms before the door even closed. It was exactly how I had fallen into my mother's arms through that same doorway the year before. After the initial tears, we made it to the living room. We sat on the large green couch in silence. And when words finally came, we talked.

He took my letter when I left and assured me that he'd keep checking in so we'd know he was safe. As I drove home, I was in awe. For a relationship that was, as my sister very aptly called it "surface level" for so many years, we'd experienced some intense and vulnerable feelings together. I was proud of us.

I was proud of not only feeling, but being brave enough to dip my toe into facing what I was feeling. Then I honestly expressed my feelings in my letter, which some might even call dealing with them. Look at me go! Feeling and dealing. It was a whole new experience for me, and I was finding that I had gratitude even in these moments of pain.

Jen Sincero warned of the BS, but Paulo Coelho shared in *The Alchemist* another lesson:

"What you still need to know is this: before a dream is realized, the Soul of the World tests everything that has been learned along the way. It does this not because it is evil, but so that we can, in addition to realizing our dreams, master the lessons we've learned as we've moved toward that dream."

I realized that the recent struggles at work, at home, and in my family were not there to stop my growth journey. The struggles were opportunities to apply what I'd learned. Opportunities to try new behaviors. They were gifts from God.

But even though I could see them as gifts, they were emotionally draining gifts. And I was exhausted. I felt raw. And even though I'd gotten out one good round of tears thanks to Cassie's forced-hug-with-love, I still felt restless.

That's when I started spending more time with my friend, Janine. Janine was a friend that showed up in the exact right season of my life. She was a petite little thing who didn't have much to say but had listening ears for miles. She also had a passion for yoga and helped me find the quiet and peaceful walls of our local yoga studio. I relished the solitude on my mat where I allowed my mind to be quiet and still.

I started going regularly, enjoying the hot bikram yoga where I could sweat and let a few random tears trickle down. There, no one seemed to care. Everyone was focused on themselves, which was great because I had enough to focus on. It was a lot like therapy, even though I was still chilling on Jules' couch pretty frequently, too.

Even though I'd leave the studio feeling peaceful, within hours darker feelings crept back in and ran strong. I kept asking Jules how to get myself to cry. I knew I needed to; I could feel it. But I was struggling to get beyond misty eyes and a burning throat. I didn't want to have to keep bringing in friends to prod my tears out of me. Jules listened intently, then gave me another gem of wisdom.

"Go somewhere safe. Then let your mind go where it would never want to go, and there you'll find the tears."

She sounded like Yoda or Mr. Miyagi. My logical brain couldn't figure out how to decipher her counseling code talk. But on October 15, 2016, as I sat in the cemetery on a sunny, blue-skied day, it started to make sense.

October 15th would always have a firm grip on my heart. It was the day that my cousin, JoAnn, died at the age of 36 from a tragic and all too quick fight with cancer.

I'd grown up with JoAnn. She was eight years older than me. Our moms were sisters and best friends. I watched JoAnn go to prom in a puffy-sleeved light blue dress in the '80s. I rode in the car with my parents through an ice storm to watch her graduate from college. I watched her get married and then have babies. I watched her and loved her. She was funny, sarcastic, and always so wise.

I had driven to the hospital to visit her in her final weeks. It was my closest experience with death, watching someone I loved fight a disease they were powerless over. She fought so hard for her life. The life she didn't want to leave. The two boys she didn't want to go through life without their mother. But her fight came to an end on October 15, 2007.

JoAnn had been gone so long, but I still missed her so much. I wasn't much of a cemetery person, so I hadn't made it a habit to come by and visit. But this year, nine years later, something pulled me there, and I trusted my gut. I drove up, parked my car, and didn't see any other visitors.

It was just me and her.

I sat at the foot of JoAnn's gravesite. I looked at her picture on her headstone. Then, I decided it wouldn't hurt to just talk to her . . . out loud. I told her I had been through quite a bit, and I was tired. I told her I'd given BS a run for her money. I told her I hadn't stopped growing.

But then I got quiet. And I realized in that moment that I had yet to go to certain places that my heart didn't want to go—places that were still beaten and bruised. I still hadn't mourned certain losses.

I missed JoAnn and wished she was there calling me Deaner-Weiner, a horrible nickname that only she could get away with. I hated cancer. I hated that JoAnn's boys couldn't experience her love. I was sad that I'd lost my sense of who I was at some point. I wished my marriage hadn't suffered and that I hadn't made choices that hurt the man I loved. I was heartbroken that my parents were hurting and having to deal with their separation. And I was sad that my professional dreams of speaking were still only that—dreams.

I was in a safe place as I sat on the ground near JoAnn. There, I let my heart go where it didn't want to go—to all the sadness and heartbreak and despair. And sure enough, the tears fell. I sat on the dirt next to JoAnn and sobbed.

I finally understand now, Jules.

I sat in my sadness and mourned for myself and others. But as I heard wind chimes singing a song from the breeze I could only feel, I had to remember to hold tight to faith. Faith that dealing with all my feelings would eventually lead to healing at some point.

Feel. Deal. Heal. That's the mantra, right?

And while it didn't feel like it and at times I wondered if it ever would, the tattoo I'd gotten exactly one year before to the day continued to express the sentiment I longed to feel. Just 365 days before, I had walked into Mom's Tattoos in Austin with my mom, my sister, and JoAnn's parents, my aunt and uncle, to honor JoAnn. We'd decided to make the day about love instead of loss.

We knew full well JoAnn was laughing her butt off at us up there in Heaven. We were an odd-looking bunch, each walking out with a different permanent mark on our bodies as a reminder of JoAnn's life.

As I sat in the cemetery and cried one year later, I wrapped my right hand around my left side. Under my hand, forever inked on the skin over my ribs in JoAnn's writing were the words *"All Is Well."* And in my writing underneath hers were the words *"With My Soul."*

All is well with my soul.

Maybe one day, all would be well. Free of these sad, darker times. Or perhaps even right here, in these moments of sadness, all was exactly as it should be in my soul. I didn't need to resign myself to the fact that life would have its difficulties; rather, I needed to embrace them for the opportunities they presented. I was finally grasping that the growth journey towards a stronger, happier, healthier me was never intended to come easy.

Life was full of ups and downs, highs and lows. That's why

we had the full emotional spectrum to experience them. I just had to find a safe space to release them. It was time to be open to living, and learning, and feeling through whatever came my way, and that would have to be well with my ever-growing soul!

Chapter 9

Campfire Clarity

"I MADE FIRE!"

I shot a picture of the roaring fire along with my proclamation to my husband with pride! But the picture didn't do it justice.

It was late December 2016, and while hunting season was usually "boy time," I tagged along this year. Every time I came to the deer lease, I experienced a calming stillness. Time seemed to slow down as we made our way through a few gates down the dirt roads to make it to camp.

The thought of having some alone time out in nature was just what I needed. So after the boys headed out for the afternoon hunt, I had over three hours by myself to relish the quiet. Silence had a beautiful hum to it with barely a sound to be heard, except maybe a bird or a breeze through the trees.

I had piled up all the wood I'd needed, doused it with way more lighter fluid than was probably necessary, and sparked the flame. I watched as it grew and spread. I had made fire, and it was beautiful. Beautiful enough to brag about to my hubby through text. Just like the picture didn't do the fire's beauty justice, it also couldn't share the comforting heat. The warmth I could feel on my face and legs matched the colors of the sunset that would soon fight for my attention.

As the fire glowed in reds, oranges, and hints of blue, I sat cozied up to it with pencil and paper in hand, ready to reflect on 2016 and dream for 2017. I heard crackles and pops as I flashed back to my year of Fearless Growth. With the Universe's help, I'd grown each and every day, moment by fearless moment, thanks to the lessons thrown my way. What a year it had been.

2017 was just days away though, and it was time to decide what my new mantra would be. As I stared into the flames, it was hard to believe that in only a couple of months, I'd be taking a break. A long break. The break I had known I needed but had to gather serious amounts of courage to ask for.

The voice in my mind had started whispering: *You need a break.*

A break sounded great. But hearing a voice and actually knowing what to do with it were two different things. Of course, I wanted a break. Who wouldn't? My workload was heavy, my family was still working through difficult conversations and transitions, and I was continuing to try and find some resolve as to what I'd do next with myself and my work.

I was almost a full year and a half into my personal growth journey, and while I had given the firm notice of my soul searching, there was still no clear answer on what that would look like. Did I want to leave? If so, when? If I stayed, did I want to create a new practice area? And if so, was there any need for that in the market?

So. Many. Questions.

Then one day as I sat in a room brainstorming ideas with two other firm leaders that I respected, I heard something that hit me hard and threw me off course.

"Well, I like it, but we need to try and stay away from it being a *'Dena Thing.'*"

I was taking it in, including the air quotes he'd thrown up when he'd said the phrase, "Dena Thing." There was no proposed program I'd ever called a "Dena Thing," so I didn't know what he was talking about.

My logical mind and feeling heart struggled a bit, ultimately deciding that the comment might have been intended to highlight a difference between what I, Dena, thought people needed and what the leaders of the firm thought people needed. But still, at that moment a part of me that I didn't really know was there reared up and wanted to say, "What the heck is wrong with it being a *'Dena thing?'*"

I didn't share my irritation, but my red cheeks and faster words may have given me away. A part of me was hurt. Here I was actively trying to do exactly that—*my Dena thing*—and all I heard back was that maybe it wasn't wanted or needed here. Or worse, maybe *I* was no longer wanted or needed here.

That realization was scary. Even though I had been the one to start the discussion on a possible transition, part of me wanted to pump the breaks and stop moving altogether. It was safe here. Why drive off into the unknown? Feeling like I was spinning in circles, I kept hearing that voice say, *Take a break.* I wanted to listen and acknowledge it.

I hear you. I feel you. But what would a break look like?

The answer that came back wasn't clear. Instead, it was simply to stay curious and start seeking more information.

So that's what I did. I started digging in to see if there was a sabbatical program that I could take advantage of, but there wasn't. So I made some calls to a friend and colleague in the CPA world and asked questions on sabbatical best practices—the benefits, the potential consequences, the pay structure, and so on. I took notes, read articles, and gathered up all the information I could. And armed with all that info, I took the next scary step.

JP had heard me saying that I wanted a break, but I had to go one brave step further. I had to ask if we could consider it as a real option. Knowing that we might have a couple months with no pay was scary, but on top of that, the fact that I'd ask for a break like this was foreign to him.

He was a worker bee. He came from a bloodline that worked. And they worked hard. Sabbaticals were not common in the farming community. But I knew I needed it, and I told him so. I knew it wasn't healthy for me to continue on like I was, building up stress and anxiety and gaining no clarity for our next steps. After a few conversations, he told me to go for it. I was so grateful that he could support me even if it didn't make any sense to him.

United on the home front, it was time for me to take the next step: to ask for the leave. But first, I had to prepare. I got out notecards and started writing out my thoughts. It might seem odd, but note cards were my new tool for clarity. I started using them after another partner in the firm had given me some of the best feedback I'd ever received: "Same love, Dena, less words."

His observation was on point, and I gladly accepted it. I loved words, but as I tried to explain my passions and ideas to other people in the firm without a plan, my nonstop words kept getting the best of me. And as a result, my message was getting lost. I'd taken his feedback and started honing in on what I truly wanted to say when heading into important, meaningful conversations, and I'd bring my handy, 4x6 note cards along to help.

Armed with two notecards, I walked into the meeting I had requested and scheduled with our team leader to talk about a sabbatical. She didn't know the reason for our talk but had accepted and met me on a couch in the hotel lobby of a conference we were both attending.

Even with people moving and talking all around us, I felt like we were the only people in the room. And she didn't seem to flinch when I pulled out my notecards and started talking through my prepared points.

- *I'm tired and need a break.*
- *I've been asked to come up with a plan, and I can't find clarity.*
- *I've done my homework and want to request a sabbatical.*
- *I'm asking for a leave of 6–8 weeks.*
- *I've thought through a plan that should work for us all—me, the firm, and our clients.*
- *I believe there are options on how to make it work.*
- *I really need this for myself.*
- *Thank you.*

I was terrified going into that meeting, but I shouldn't have been surprised with how the words on my notecards were received. She was kind, calm, and reassuring.

"We will figure it out."

There would have to be more meetings to nail it down, but she said we could make it happen. I'll never know what might have been going on in her mind. She was charged with making our entire team function, and my request was surely a reason for some alarm. But to me, in that vulnerable moment of asking, she was gracious.

And she continued to be over the next few weeks as we hammered out the plan, got the other partners who would step up in my absence on board, and communicated it to our team and clients. It would happen; I just had a couple months to wait until it was the right time. February 2017 would be here before we knew it; my sabbatical was officially on the horizon.

❧

The glowing sunset on the horizon that I stared into now at the deer lease brought me back to the decision at hand. What would 2017 be about? A few ideas were running through my mind, but I couldn't stop thinking about an exchange I'd had with my friend and trainer, John, when I'd called to tell him that I was going to stop working out with him.

"Man . . . okay, Dena, but you have got to find some balance."

I'd been working out with John since my daughter was 4 months old, as I was finding my way back to health after the postpartum blues began to subside. Exercise at his boot camp created a new routine and burned off stress, anxiety, and baby weight.

But now after over nine years of knowing him, after years of workouts, personal conversations, and a lot of highs and lows, I decided I needed a change. I told him that I had decided to quit working out with him and focus on yoga. I needed a different kind of bodywork and found that yoga was helping my mind stay calm throughout the recent and seemingly never-ending emotional storms.

I'd been working hard, and my body was in a place where I felt strong and fit, but my emotional stamina was huffing and puffing. My gut was telling me to go all in on a quiet, heated room with my feet squarely rooted on my mat. I couldn't fight anymore to get in a certain number of reps or lift any more weight. I couldn't compete anymore with other campers or myself to reach the finish line.

I told him as much. And he didn't fuss at me, even though I know he was disappointed. He just said I needed balance. I was walking away from his workouts for the time being, but I was also walking away with his words stuck in my head.

Balance, balance, balance.

When it came to balance, all I could imagine was a tightrope where I was teetering to the right and left, just about to plummet to the ground. But I wanted to find a solid steadiness in my core, an unwavering focus. I wanted to make it from one side to the other safe and sound.

I wanted to find balance.

I also remained fascinated with one of my top 3 fears: the loss of control (aka freedom). It had come up as one of my fears, but I had just taken a big step through that fear when I asked for my sabbatical. I'd asked for time and space to clear my mind and hopefully gain clarity. I wanted to feel free.

How could those two things—balance and freedom—go together? What might that look like? I stumbled upon it in my mind, then said it out loud.

Balanced Freedom.

It seemed to imply that I'd find some balance that I and most every other working wife and mother was seeking. But it also added an unexpected layer of freedom. Could I balance work, people, and relationships and also find the freedom to focus on me, myself, and I? I didn't know, but I was eager to find out.

And so, I decided. 2017 would be my year of *Balanced Freedom*. It felt right. I took a deep breath, wrote it down on my sheet of paper, and smiled as I watched the glow of the fire that I'd created. The sun had set, and stars were now covering the sky that had turned black.

What would God and the Universe bring my way this coming year? I didn't know, but I was calm and ready.

One month later, I listened to my calm and steady friend Janine as she instructed me. "Breathe, Dena. Don't forget to breathe."

I did as she said.

The time had finally come to walk out of the office and start my sabbatical. The team had done an excellent job. My work plate was empty. Everything was ready for the other partners to transition over during my leave. But as I sat there at my desk, a panic had come on and would not leave. It hit me like a freight train as I was about to activate my "Out of Office" automatic replies.

What if we forgot something? What if we miss something while I'm out?

The fear freight train surged on and on and on. But Janine texted me off the ledge, and I continued to breathe.

Inhale, exhale. Inhale, exhale.

Then, I clicked.

The "Out of Office" messages were on, my voicemail was set, and I walked out of the building feeling awkward, hopeful, and somewhat lighter. It was time to take off eight weeks from work. I had been counting down the days, and during all that time, people kept asking me, "What are you going to do while you're out?"

Good question. The only thing I consistently said was that no matter what, I wanted to reconnect with my kids. I'd felt that all the recent growth had pulled me away from spending focused time with them so in this time off, they would be a priority.

But other than my babies, I didn't have plans to travel the world or anything else wild or crazy. With two kiddos in elementary school and a husband still working, I'd for sure be staying local. I had a few ideas of grandeur, including little things like writing a book, working out twice a day, eating super healthy, and losing some of the emotional weight that I'd packed on. I mean really, what else was I going to do with my time?

The first week or so I treated myself to a spa day and even surprised my husband with a quick getaway to a neat new hotel in nearby San Antonio. He had to head back the next morning to get to work, but I stayed because I could! I lounged in a hot bath, then went and sat by the river and watched a little turtle trying to climb up the bank for almost an hour. Why not? I had time on my hands.

Having hours to do with as I pleased and zero immediate responsibilities was amazing. No emails to respond to, no meetings to get to, no decisions to make! It was a freedom I hadn't known. So, I sat. I sat by the water and watched that turtle toil away. His work became my work. I cheered him on (not out loud, thank goodness). I texted JP to let him know what I was up to.

"Oh my, you're talking to turtles. Maybe you did need a break."

Poor turtle never did make it up the rocks. The little guy kept slipping and falling right back to where he started. I knew that feeling. Working so hard but not getting anywhere. But he succeeded in entertaining me. And I had succeeded in doing something simply because it made me happy.

After that getaway, my time off became both fascinating and a bit disorienting off the bat. At least my mornings were predictable. I'd get up, put on my favorite robe, and head to the kitchen. I took over making lunches, which had previously been my husband's task since I was always getting ready to go to work. After breakfasts were eaten and lunches packed, I either drove the kids to school or walked them to the neighbor to carpool.

Some days I read, some days I met up with girlfriends, some days I went to a movie. Other days I'd run boring errands. There was no one there to tell me what to do or where to go. I didn't sit down and actively try and plan out my next steps. I just lived. And one day, I purged. I loaded up bags of things to donate and felt so much lighter. (Even though I later realized, I accidentally purged my wedding rings. Oopsies!)

While I may have lost my wedding rings, one of the things I found early in my growth journey and hadn't let go of was listening to the voices in my head. Whispers were telling me yet again that I needed another girls' trip. Or more accurately, a girl trip. Solo and singular. Something inside of me wanted to go away . . . alone!

My Meant for More journey had been an intentional one so far. I had purposefully learned new things, made changes in my life, and worked to make healthier choices. I had stripped my life down layer by layer and was putting each one back on as they felt right—my marriage, my children, my friends. Now, I wanted space around me (and only me!) to dabble in what that kind of freedom would feel like, and even more, what it might have to offer me.

There's a saying I love: "The cure for anything is salt water— tears, sweat, or the sea." I'd started to believe it was true. I'd taken to the sweaty goodness of hot yoga and the hot-faced messy crying that was coming more easily to me. What I'd been missing though was the ocean! So with only a few weeks left in my sabbatical, I planned a trip to the beach.

It would be my maiden voyage—my first-ever solo vacation. I had never gone anywhere away from my family by myself. I was nervous at first broaching the topic with JP because again; farmers aren't known for taking sabbaticals and for sure not going on solo trips to the beach. But after a few conversations, he took it in stride.

Funny enough, when I was packing to go, he seemed nervous for me. It wasn't like some romantic comedy movie; he didn't give me a heartwarming speech about chasing the wind and waves. That wasn't his style. But he loved me, and his love trickled out in small reminders and questions.

"Are you sure you know how to get there?"

"Dena, don't you want to take this ice chest instead?"

"What about this beach chair? That one has the broken arm."

His support came through in his own way, and with it, I knew I was loved. Armed with that (and the better ice chest and beach chair of course), I was ready to go.

I made my way toward Port Aransas, Texas where I would spend the next three days and two nights at one of our favorite beach resorts. I was reminded of all that's awesome about being on the open road alone: blue sky for miles and no one to tell me to turn down the volume of my all-too-girly playlist!

When I got into town, I stopped at the local grocery store and got more snacks to add to my small stash in the ice chest. I checked into my room, unpacked my things—two or three books that I'd been reading, three or four of my all-time favorite chick flicks, and no plan—and then opened the sliding glass door to the balcony.

And there it was.

I took in the endless ocean view, the sun and the waves and the salty smell. I had no idea what I would do next on my trip. I figured it would be a beautiful free flow from what sounded good to me at the moment to what seemed good to me in the next. And in this moment, I just wanted to be near the water to hear the waves coming in and out.

Over the next couple of days, life was simple. Read books, watch movies, lounge by the ocean. Check, check, check! I was officially and unapologetically enjoying my time alone. But on my last night there, I'd had enough simple. It was time for a challenge. I had hard work to do if I chose to be brave enough to do it.

One of the movies I had packed was *The Notebook*. A fantastic film made all the better by Ryan Gosling's presence but also a movie based on a book by Nicholas Sparks. It was known for making people feel all of the feels. Strong selection for a girly movie some might say, but to me, it wasn't just a girly movie. It was a gutsy challenge to look yet another dark memory in the face and see who would blink first.

The Notebook had been with me on one of my darkest days.

It was another bad day during my postpartum battle after my daughter was born. I kept telling myself and my mom that if I could just feel, if I could just cry, then surely, I would get better. So, I made a plan to watch *The Notebook*. Why? Because it made sense. Who could watch that movie and not cry? I had taken both kids to my mom's house. She'd agreed to watch them while I went home to have that good cry.

It was dark and empty in my house and my heart that day. Hopeful and alone, I put the DVD in and hit play. I watched the movie. But nothing happened. I had no tears. I had no quivering chin, no burning throat. I was numb. I was broken. And I knew that wasn't good; *I* wasn't good.

What seemed like a good idea at the time was to call my then-boss, Julia, at work. Julia was a woman who had grown near and dear to my heart, and as I started to panic, she came into my racing mind. With dry eyes, I called her. She answered, and my rant began. During my postpartum struggles, these rants were part of the norm. I would talk in circles, allowing the snowball of my irrational thoughts to build as they screamed down the mountain.

She listened as I let my words flow like a dark stream of consciousness.

I tried to watch a sad movie . . . I needed to feel . . . But I didn't feel . . . That's not good, Julia! What will I be like when I come back to work? Will you fire me? If you fire me, will we lose the house? And if we lose the house, what will happen then?

And now here I was over nine years later, ready to challenge myself to that movie again. All these years later, I was still craving the same things that I was on that dark day. I still wanted to feel love and connection—not just at a surface level but way down deep.

I put in the DVD and hit play. The movie hadn't changed. I knew what would happen at the end. I knew who I'd be rooting for the whole movie. Ryan Gosling was still beautiful. The rain scene was still ridiculously romantic. She would still forget her family and not know that it was the love of her life visiting her and telling her stories. And they would still hold hands and close their eyes as the birds flew away.

But this time, something was different in me. Something new happened. My chin started to quiver. My eyes got misty, and my throat burned like fire. And this time, I didn't stop it. I was ready to give up and give in. I doubt I could have stopped even if I'd tried. The well was going to run over. I let go, and I sobbed. The tears gushed out, and it was amazing! What would have been no big deal for so many was a fabulous full circle for me.

It was a full circle of wanting so desperately to feel things deeply, and I'd made it. Feeling for me had once been lost, but now, it was found. Not feeling was what I had known and clung to.

Don't feel because it's scary. Don't lose control.

The old thinking had served its purpose, protecting me in ways that I had needed when I was a child. But I was no longer a child. I was a grown woman, and I was ready to feel deeply. The movie might have been the spark, but the tears were about going to the places my heart hadn't wanted to go back to—times when I'd lost love and connection with myself and my own babies. I had done some major feeling and dealing. Now, lo and behold, I found healing in those salty tears.

The calm and peace that followed my cry was a gift. I slept hard, woke up feeling refreshed, and made myself bacon and eggs. Then I sat there quietly staring at the salty sea. I missed my husband. I missed my children. It was time to go back to them. And I was ready. I had finally experienced some real-life healing. I was going to be able to let many of those dark, bad-day memories scar over so I could move on.

As I prepared to return to work the following week, I realized I was ready. I missed my work friends. Distance had, in fact, made my heart grow fonder, but my sabbatical helped me find a few other things that I was fond of in my career. I liked the structure of a work day. I liked being part of a team and feeling like I was contributing.

But as much as I was ready to go back, I was finally able to say with clarity that I would walk away one day. I would need to chase my dreams outside the walls of the firm. And even more than that, I had an end date in mind. I'd work to find a way to transition out by the end of 2018. I didn't have the specific steps figured out, but I knew for sure that I'd be leaving and would tell them when I returned.

So was my sabbatical worth it? Was it worth the fear to ask, worth the guts to then actually take it, and worth facing all sorts of unknowns while in the middle of it? Heck yeah, it was! I hadn't checked off many boxes of what I thought I was going to do. (Two workouts a day? Funny, Dena!) But I had asked for and then took the time I needed to be still.

And in that time—in that free space I'd given myself—I was able to offload the weight of emotional baggage I'd been hauling around with me for years. Each and every emotion I'd walked through had been worth it. I was proud of myself. The stillness hadn't stopped my forward progression. Instead, it had steadied me, providing me a sense of balance and the freedom to explore.

And in the end, it had given me a more definite sense of direction as the road kept opening up right in front of me.

Chapter 10

Teamwork Makes the Dream Work

I WALKED INTO THE OFFICE and exchanged pleasantries with two partners I worked with as we settled in. The lead partner of our audit practice was sitting across from me behind her desk, and I swear she started to sit up taller. The posture when someone is preparing to deliver something big. The partner sitting next to me in the other chair didn't make direct eye contact with me, focusing on the bearer of whatever news was about to come. The intensity in the room was palpable.

"Dena, we realized that we haven't stopped to ask you: What do you really want?"

She kept talking—talking about how now that we had a partner lined up to be my successor to take over and lead the practice, I could leave earlier. It was early August 2017, and they were already thinking of the year ahead and how all the pieces of the practice scheduling puzzle fit together. She said it might be easier for everyone actually, but there was no pressure. Her words droned on and on, covered by alarm bells ringing in my head. So many thoughts and responses bubbled up into my mind.

Wait, what do you mean what do I want? We all know I want to leave, and we're planning for that. We've agreed to me leaving on December 31, 2018. Sure, it's over a year away, but it will happen.

She repeated the question.

"Dena, what do you want to do?"

I went speechless.

Literally, I could not speak; nothing would come out of my mouth. I was a woman of many, many words. I was going to launch a business that I'd decided to call Dena Speaks, for goodness sakes! But now, I was speechless.

When I had regained some ability to speak, I rambled out all the thoughts racing through my mind.

"Well, the timeframe we'd agreed to is good for my family. We'd have insurance, and it gives us a safety net financially as I build up my business."

"Right, but Dena, if insurance is your first thought, we don't know how you are going to truly be happy while you are here. Again, no pressure, but just know that whenever you want to go, we can make it work."

What the heck?!

My mind was reeling. We'd already had several meetings, each with its own twists and turns, but we'd finally nailed down a few things. I would leave, and I would leave at the end of 2018. We had a confirmed successor who would take over my practice. We had figured those things out. We had a plan.

Why were they trying to change the plan?

I was not prepared for this new line of questioning, and it shut me down. I tried to respond to them, but my words were gone again. I couldn't finish a stinking sentence. It was like when Dr. Maynard punched me with the, "Maybe you're not a passionate person," comment all over again. And then, I started to cry. Just a little mist in the eyes, but still.

Jeez, Dena.

I apologized for my emotional reaction. I told them I heard what they were saying, but moving my exit date up any sooner had not been on my radar, and it was throwing my control-freak self into a little panic.

"Sure, it sounds great to leave sooner, but it's not what JP and I agreed on. I appreciate this little nudge you're giving me to make sure I'm still good with things. But I'll have to talk with JP."

I walked out of the room with a racing heart and an echoing in my mind.

What do you want, Dena?

I'd agreed to come back to them in a couple of weeks with an update. I walked straight to my car where I texted a small group of my closest girlfriends. I shared that I needed prayers, good vibes, or anything else they could send my way because this conversation felt like such a big deal to me, and it would for sure be a big deal to my husband.

I didn't reach out to JP. I sat with their question all day on my own.

What did I want?

I knew what I really wanted was to leave earlier. To try and get both feet on one side of the dang imaginary line I was straddling—one foot in corporate world and one in entrepreneurship. But I couldn't give them that answer because I knew I couldn't make that decision alone.

Even though I was all about freedom and chasing my dreams, I had a partner at home. Marriage was a legal and licensed union in the eyes of the State, and you know, a vow before God and all. But it was also a business. And the business of marriage contained certain financial contracts that I could not and would not change the terms on unless he was on board.

This was a big conversation that I knew I'd have to have with JP, and I didn't know if I was ready. I had to hone in on myself first before bringing it to him. I would talk to him; I had proved that I could. We'd made it this far, hadn't we? But I'd have to sit on this one for just a bit longer. So, I went the rest of the day without sharing about the meeting with JP. I decided it could and should wait.

It seemed like the right decision at the time because I knew we were driving into this decision in what felt like a bit of a fog. We were both gripping the steering wheel with caution taking over our instincts. Since we'd originally agreed that I would leave the firm, there had been a mounting tension. There wasn't a specific event where JP and I got off track. Rather I had voices in my own mind that were making me question the path we were on and if I still had a ready and willing copilot.

And as had become normal in my world, there continued to be voices in my mind that felt and sounded so real—so loud and clear. In particular there were two instances where I received messages—one that shook me to the core and the other that seemed to be a gift from God to get me back on the road.

The first came to me just as I had started feeling that JP and I were not on the same page—that I wasn't supported by him in ways that I knew I wanted and needed as we prepared for my work transition. Not that I knew exactly what I wanted and needed, except some sense of intense support that I could trust and hold tight to. But as I was holding my husband tight in a very intimate moment one night, I was not expecting what happened next.

I heard five words loud and clear: *I wish you knew me.*

I looked around thinking for sure JP had heard it too, but he didn't acknowledge anything. Only I had heard the voice, and in a moment where we were about as vulnerable as you could get, the string of words ran wild in my mind.

I wish you knew me.

Did it mean he wished I knew him? Or did I wish he knew me? I mean, my husband knew me. And I knew him. We'd been together for more years than we had not at this point in our lives. What could that mean?

I wish you knew me.

It left me unsettled, not only that night but for days and weeks to come. As I continued to pick it apart by myself, with Jules, and then with God, a few things became clearer.

Just days after hearing the voice—*I wish you knew me*—I was getting my church in through a podcast on the way to work. Luckily, we could now get to God at any time through any device. That morning, I was listening through my car speakers to Pastor Jason with Austin New Church give a message titled "To Know Or To Be Known By God."

The sermon covered Galatians 4:8-11. In the context of the biblical story, he was breaking apart the concept of knowing someone versus being known by them. The sermon was timely and relatable not only because of the whisper I was deciphering but because of my personal connection to God. Part of my personal growth over the last few months and now almost years included growth in my faith.

I didn't just want to know of or about God; I wanted to be known by Him. And as I'd grown emotionally and intellectually, I'd also grown spiritually. I felt certain that I was in fact known by God. I had become resolute in my faith that God was not only with me on my journey toward my dreams, but that the ideas and passions had been divinely planted there.

As a result of all of the seeking I had been doing in my

own personal growth journey, I had finally found answers that I trusted to be true. I believed that I had a God-given passion for inspiring others and sharing my story. The unique life mission that I'd written poolside for myself over a year ago was still right on. They had become truths that I could no longer ignore.

Sermons were meant to make you think, right? Well, that sermon podcast had done its job. It helped me buckle up tight in my faith and personal relationship with God. I took the lessons Pastor Jason was sharing and extended them beyond me and God and into my next most important relationship.

I didn't just want JP to know me; I wanted to be known by him. I wanted to be deeply and personally understood, loved, cared for, and supported. I wanted to feel like he had a gentle hand on the small of my back, not pushing me but instead letting me know he was there, ready to gently nudge me forward if I needed it or to catch me if I fell. I wanted him to truly understand what I wanted to do and why I wanted to venture into the great unknown.

I wanted JP buckled up by my side. Buckled up with faith in me and my calling.

I wish you knew me.

I was too scared to talk to JP about that first voice. I don't know why; he'd proven he could hang. He'd gotten on board with me leaving. But something about how we talked about the work I dreamed of made it feel like it was a business transaction he understood rather than a very personal decision he supported me in. That seemed to be the line I wasn't ready to cross over in conversation.

Instead of talking to him though, I kept it to myself and let my mind get the best of me.

Maybe he doesn't really understand me?
Maybe he isn't really on board.
Maybe he doesn't think I can do it.

The tires of my mind spun out, leaving me feeling anxious. But I kept my mouth shut tight.

The second voice made her appearance while we were on our final family vacation of summer 2017, just a few weeks after the first voice showed up in my mind and took center stage. We were staying in a perfect little cabin in the mountains just outside Red Lodge, Montana. Mountains, crisp air, a stream running by the side of the cabin—it was definitely a place of peace and refuge. And way better than the 100-degree days of sweat and humidity we'd left behind at home!

One day while the boys were off trying fly fishing, my daughter and I found ourselves perched up high on horses. We'd found a place called Whispering Winds Horse Adventures and decided to have a little mother-daughter adventure. But as we talked with Linda, the owner who had a short and weathered stature, and Dave, her tall, lanky boyfriend and trusty side kick, we learned it would be an easy ride given her horses were old and calm—just what she needed as most of her work was with autistic children.

So, as I sat in my saddle on my horse, enjoying the very slow and methodical clip-clop-clip-clop walk along the very safe, well-worn paths of Whispering Winds, I hadn't expected to hear an actual whisper. And at first, it seemed pretty straightforward.

You are capable of more.

Of course, I thought I was capable of a slightly faster pace on my horse, but who really cared. Was that whisper-worthy? Did I need to know that or hear that right now for some reason? I started the mental breakdown.

You? You mean me? Do you mean I am capable of more?

Was it a challenge or just a statement of fact?

You are capable of more.

After our ride was over, I got to chat with Linda and learned that she and Dave had met online. This woman who also had a Pepto-Bismol pink house continued to surprise me. Who would have thought? But as she rambled on about how different their lives had been—she'd been raised and worked on the farm, he'd lived and worked on computers in the city—she landed on an important fact. A fact I didn't know I needed to hear.

"Even though we have lots of differences, in the things that matter, we're on the same page."

I pumped my mental breaks for a second. The whispers were all coming together with Linda's words. I was starting to get it. This take on her relationship was the kicker. I had come into this family vacation time with an unsettled fear in my heart. A fear that I'd still not broached with JP.

But her matter of fact statement made me realize that I had a choice to make. Do I hold my tongue and avoid the deeper conversation with him? This had always been our M.O. If I ignored the doubts and fears, then I'd also ignore my sincere desire to connect with JP on a different level. There were risks, but it didn't take me long to reach a decision. I couldn't ignore things anymore. If I wanted what I said I wanted, I had to go for it.

The potential pain of not speaking far outweighed the risks. After all, Dena Speaks couldn't just be a catchy business name; it had to be my new M.O. It only took a few weeks for me to get the chance to put all the things I'd learned from these whispers into action. And when the time came, I held tight to the hushed truth I'd heard: *You are capable of more.*

"Dena, what do you want to do?"

I had waited all day, thinking about that question and wondering what JP might think. When he got home, I asked if he'd join me on the back porch. As we rocked side by side in matching rocking chairs, I shared what happened in the meeting. As easy as the rocking chairs were going back and forth, so was my husband's wall of defense. I could see the bricks of surprise, fear, anger, and who knows what else piling up from his dirty boots all the way up to his head.

"What do you think?"

I waited for his response to break through his heavy brooding silence.

"Just tell me what you decide, and we'll figure it out."

I'd spent the entire day circling the issue, and all I got back was a quick, one-sentence response. My cheeks flushed with frustration, and my rocker stopped rocking. I failed to stop and think about how much time he might need to process it. I'd had all day for goodness sakes. I forgot that. All I knew was that in that moment, his response wasn't going to cut it with me.

"Well, I won't accept that response. You *will* share with me how this really makes you feel and what you really think. I can wait. I will wait."

He met my demand with more silence that I decided to fill.

"JP, I'm not the kind of person who would walk in and be like, 'Surprise, honey, I quit my job today!' I need you to be involved in this with me, and I am going to make sure that you are."

Who was I and where had the old Dena gone? Look at me go! I would have fled from this type of emotional dialogue just months ago (shoot, even days ago), but I was capable of more, right? I could do hard things. I could have hard conversations with my husband. I could wait.

And in this case, I was going to have to wait. Because he made me.

It was excruciating waiting even the few minutes (which felt more like hours) before he finally spoke up.

"You really want to know?"

"Yes, I do."

"Fine, yeah . . . So, I'm scared."

And then his floodgates opened, and all the scary possibilities he'd been holding back flowed out.

What if this . . .?
What if that . . .?
I can't be sure that this . . .
I don't know if that . . .

That's when I finally saw that we agreed on one thing: We were both scared. Leaving the security of a well-paying career with benefits was scary. We both knew that all of his work was risk-based; there were zero guarantees in the world of farming and agriculture. He'd been successful in creating his own insurance agency as his complimentary career, but I was the consistent, steady earner. I provided our family financial stability. Walking away from that was scary. On those facts, we completely agreed.

Being on the same page when it came to our fears was a good place to start, but we couldn't get to the same page on the real issue at hand. *How soon could I leave?* That was the decision on the table. If nothing changed, we had almost 15 months to prepare. But my heart was saying, *The sooner, the better*, and his logic and need for security were saying, *The longer, the better*. We had ground to cover.

I offered something new for us this time—something we hadn't tried before in these important conversations. I suggested that instead of deciding right then, that we meet back up in a few days to check back in on it. Allow ourselves time alone to process then put our heads back together. He agreed, and we went our separate ways.

Individually, we started chipping away at the options, the questions, and the potential consequences. We prayed and talked to friends, and I whipped up a spreadsheet or two. Then a few days later, we kept our commitment and met back to share where we were in our thinking. We followed that pattern again and again.

In each conversation, we started to consider different, earlier end dates. We began to talk more openly about our finances, which had not previously been an open discussion in our home. Not that we'd made poor choices financially or were avoiding anything, it just hadn't been top priority. But now, our financial security and the need to discuss it had risen in the ranks. It was a topic that we needed to grow more comfortable with and now had the opportunity to do so.

And then, there was a hurricane. A real-life, beast of a hurricane, and they called him Harvey. Amidst what already felt like an emotional, intellectual, and spiritual hurricane swirling through my house, there was one with devastating floods and deathly destruction hitting our state and close to home. We were fortunate to only experience heavy rains, but since the fields were too wet, JP was homebound.

We were stuck at home and stuck needing to make a decision on when I'd make my leap. It was all I could focus on. And for days it felt like we were getting nowhere. One day I'd think we were about to agree, then the next I'd feel like we were back to square one. One night after I shared the position we found ourselves in with my sister in law, she asked, "What does your gut say?"

She asked it like it was that simple. My gut said to leave in February, just one year after my sabbatical and only five months from then. That was ten months earlier than the 15 months we'd planned.

But it wasn't that simple because my gut also told me that there was a more severe crisis brewing on top of the number of months on a countdown calendar. For me, the simple question of when I'd leave had evolved into a much more complex question of whether JP knew *why* I had to leave. *I wish you knew me* had turned into a far more important cry for a personal resolution.

My need to negotiate a date had turned into a need to feel truly known by my husband. His resistance to an earlier end date was interpreted by me as a lack of understanding of *who I was* and *what I was called to do*. This was a complexity that I hadn't shared with him and had only just admitted to myself. It mattered so much to me because I felt like I knew and respected who he was and what he felt called to do. And that had not been an easy task for me.

Truth was, I had been jealous of my husband for years— jealous of the fact that he had found his passion for farming so young. He could remember finding his fascination and love with dirt, seeds, and tractors when he was an eight-year-old boy. And it stuck with him.

His family told me when we were dating that our lives

would revolve around seasons and the weather. I heard it in my teens, but living and experiencing it as a growing adult had been another thing. I'd grown resentful of my husband's passions over the years and had avoided expressing the loneliness that comes with being a farmer's wife.

There was also a silent, unspoken sadness knowing that I was not his first love. Farming and all that came with it beat me to his heart, and it hurt that I would never feel like his first or even second priority. But I knew that was part of his God-given DNA, and I would never ask him to stop or walk away from it. I just wouldn't.

Keeping these things silent had been a part of our growing disconnection prior to our fall out. But in our mutual recommitment and rebuilding, I had intentionally focused much of my therapy work on these things over the last couple of years. I was trying to separate my feeling, dealing, and healing work on that from our current situation, but I couldn't ignore it altogether.

Just nights away from my scheduled follow up meeting at work, I couldn't hold it back anymore. I had to honor what my insides were telling me. I had to share that all the discussions and the decision at hand were more than me just wanting an earlier end date; it was about me wanting my husband to see me for who I believed God intended me to be.

Just like I believed God put a passion for growing things in his heart, I believed God had given me a passion for growing other people's hope and potential! I didn't know what my new career would look like, how much money I'd make, or how long it would take me to build up a business. I didn't have those answers. But I did know that I needed JP to love me. I needed him to be willing to sacrifice the security of having all the answers. I needed him to have faith in me, in us, and in what I saw as God's plan. I needed him to have faith that we would, in fact, figure out whatever life might throw our way. I needed his trust. I needed him to be on my team.

This was my life and my career—a decision that was all about me—but I wanted a partner in this dream of mine. I wanted to feel free, but freedom had a new meaning for me; it was the ability to stand alone *and* have close relationships. I'd found this definition of freedom in the book, *Conscious Loving* by Gay and Kathlyn Hendricks, and I loved it. That's what I wanted. I wanted to take control of my life's decisions, but I also wanted my husband, the one I chose to share life with, on board beside me.

So as he sat in his recliner, lounging back and holding a pillow in his lap, I decided it was time. As the weather man talked about the latest hurricane news in the background, I moved to perch on the end of my seat leaning in towards JP.

"This is more than just about when I leave, JP. I need you to really understand that I feel like I am called to do this."

My throat got tight and burned as I tried to hold back tears.

"I would never ask you to turn away from farming. But that is what I feel like you're asking me to do. I want you to believe . . . No, I *need* you to believe in me and what I feel certain I am supposed to go try and do."

I told him about the whispers and that I believed we were capable of making smart decisions along the way. And after sharing all these things with him through even more tears, I felt lighter, even freer. I could breathe. I'd shared my truth.

He listened more than he responded. He kept his eyes on mine as they got misty and overflowed. There were no calming words or persistent reassurances. But for once, his response (or lack of response) wasn't my focus. It didn't seem to matter as much. What mattered was that I had shared my truth. I had honestly expressed myself.

I'd been nudged by a simple, caring question: *But what do you want, Dena?* And with that loving punch in the gut, I'd not only found answers to questions about what I wanted but also whether I was willing to admit what I wanted to myself and others. I'd opened myself up to the vulnerable, everyday bravery that it took me to get to know myself better and reaffirm the calling placed in my heart, and then, I'd shared it with the one I loved most.

That one caring question posed by leaders of my firm had given me the chance to choose what kind of partnership I wanted in my marriage: one that was closed and fearful or one that was open and trusting. And in the end, that one question forced our hand and made us decide if my leap would be sooner rather than later. That one question was a reality check and a gift of opportunity for me and my husband to grow together.

Finally, on what seemed to be a very fitting Labor Day morning, September 4, 2017, my husband and I reached a conclusion. We'd worked hard. We'd asked questions, and we'd given answers where we could. We'd inched our way toward each other month by month. We'd even had some fun, getting creative in thinking of ways to provide us both with the security we longed for.

Each of us individually and together had worked to better understand and calm both our personal fears and those that impacted our marriage. And we'd agreed to trust each other and have faith that we could work as a team as we both worked toward our individual, God-given passions. We didn't agree to all these things verbally or explicitly. But, as we stood in our kitchen that morning, there was a new sense of calm and confidence you could feel coming from us both.

Man, I was proud of us.

We looked each other in the eyes that Labor Day morning to do a final check that we were finally on the same page.

"So, February 2nd?"

"Yup, February 2nd."

We had our decision. And, like any good teammates might do, we smiled, reached up, and gave each other a high five!

Chapter 11

Goodbye and Thank You for Coming

"AND WHAT WOULD YOU LIKE TO BE CELEBRATED for, Mrs. Dena Jansen?"

Her kind voice spoke to me through the phone line. I was sitting in a client's office covered in fluorescent lights in Austin. She was calling from sunny San Diego. She, was Carri, my coach—my life, professional, business, whatever I wanted and needed her to be coach. We'd only had five calls, each an hour-long, and this was one of her questions every time.

"What would you like to celebrate?"

My answer came back short and sweet, "I'm smiling."

That's what I wanted to celebrate.

"I'm smiling, Carri."

Her answer came back short and sweet too, "I get that."

So here we were on September 25, 2017, having a coaching call and celebrating my smile. This call was only weeks after JP and I had made the big decision for our team, high-fiving our way into the most significant, intentional life shift that we'd ever experienced. It was also only one week—seven crazy days after our last coaching call—when I had not been smiling. On that call, I'd been near panic.

The week before had been heavy. Over the span of one short week, I'd balanced both personal and professional losses that had hit me hard and left me wanting to pull over, stop the car, and turn the hazards on. And it all started just one Monday before.

I was sitting in a dark office on the phone with Carri that day. I was giving her updates on my day and shared that as soon as we were done with our call, I'd walk across the hall and share with the entire partner group that I would be leaving in a matter of months. And if we stuck to the communication schedule we'd agree to, I would then share the same news with the whole firm later the same week.

I was trying to prepare my thoughts for the partner meeting, but I was also preoccupied waiting on any word on my Paw Paw. My 90-year-old grandfather, who we all called Paw Paw, had gone into the hospital the week before. He'd had surgery, which was scary at his age. He'd fared well at first but then had some relapses. I was trying to process it all as best I could—saying goodbye to a firm I loved and waiting to see if I'd have to do the same with a grandfather I loved. I was feeling really over-whelmed, so the coaching call was a saving grace.

Carri must have been able to sense my angst and asked that we stop for a second and take some deep breaths. Why was it that I had to be reminded by other people to breathe when I was struggling? I guess I didn't care; I'd take the reminder to breathe however I could get it. The breaths slowed my heart and my mind, and I was grateful. I needed to focus. I wanted to be able to communicate my plans to the partners with calm and clarity.

She asked that I take a second to write down what I wanted to share in the partner meeting and what I wanted to feel like when I walked out after it was over. We'd not done one of these visualization exercises before, so it was new to me, but I went with it. I jotted down quickly what I wanted to express—my deepest gratitude to the firm for all it had meant to me and a quick recap on what I planned to do with Dena Speaks. I wrote down what I wanted to feel—loved, and supported, and maybe even have a little fun.

I imagined it in my mind. I wrote it on another small note-card, and then I walked in an hour later and made sure I sat right next to my dear friend, Sara, who I made promise not to let me cry. And guess what? I didn't cry. Well, not too much. I went down my list of things to share from my notecard, and I saw smiles. I only went rogue once and found myself and others laughing at whatever I'd added in. As I walked out, I walked into a hug from the same man who had been leery of a "Dena thing" just months before. He said he loved my business name and was excited for this next step for me.

I felt supported and loved. Leaving this firm was going to be hard not only because of the financial security it provided my family but because of the amazing people who walked its halls. The birth of my new reality would require me to let go of and allow this part of my professional journey to only be seen in my rearview mirror. Releasing my grip was going to be hard. But sharing with the partner group was yet another step in letting this firm go. And each time I shared my next steps with someone new, the truth set in a little deeper.

Now that the partner meeting was behind me, I had the green light to prepare the company-wide email that would tell all our people I would be leaving. But before I could craft the words to try and say all I wanted to, I had to admit that I was tired. After making it through that first communication and feeling my emotions deflate, I was pooped and decided to head home early.

Minutes before I made it home, I got the call.

It was my mom, always the calm bearer of bad news—first JoAnn, then my grandmother, Mee Maw, the year before. Now she told me that Paw Paw was gone, too. Another loss for me to feel and deal with. I'd later find out that Paw Paw took his last breath at almost the exact time that I was sharing my departing news to the partners. I knew both of these losses were coming; I knew both would happen. But as I let the news settle in, both struck me hard.

Tears fell out and rolled down my cheeks. My sunglasses covered my red, swelling eyes as I tried to stay focused on the road. I was only about ten minutes from home. I wanted to make it home, and I did, safely. Then standing alone in my kitchen, I cried harder than I may have ever cried. I let it all out. I cried and cried, and during a slight reprieve, I sent a quick text to JP that I didn't want to talk to anybody. I asked that he check in on me later. Luckily, the kids were taken care of for hours, and I had the time and space to feel.

I was safe.

I could allow myself time to mourn. And for the first time, I wasn't only allowing myself to feel it, I had even asked JP for the space that I needed to deal with it. I wasn't running from the pain. I wasn't isolating myself from it. I was welcoming the pain into my world so I could sit with it.

I cried until I couldn't cry anymore. I tried to take a nap but just ended up laying there in silence staring at the blades of the fan overhead. Then, after some Thai takeout, laughter made sense. I popped in the ever-perfect Ellen DeGeneres *Here and Now* special, and I laughed . . . and I laughed . . . and I laughed . . . until I cried again. I rode out all the waves of emotion that came with saying goodbye and losing people that I loved. Then finally, I slept.

The next morning life went on. The sun came up, and it went back down the next night. Over the next couple of days as arrangements were made for the funeral, I offered to speak and share a few words. It felt right to share my reflections to a sanctuary filled with family and friends who loved him, too.

I had important words to write and prepare in my mind to say. But even more than the words, I had to grapple with a little thing called the circle of life. Death always seemed to bring with it the opportunity to look at ourselves and our mortality in the face, and this time for me was no different.

But somehow, it felt different. When family members had died before, yes, I'd been sad, but I don't know that I genuinely felt it. "It" was what was new to me this time. I was feeling this struggle to balance the pain of loss with this ever-rising excitement for new things to come. It was weird. How could I experience both at the same time?

How could I appreciate both feelings?

I asked this very question when I sat on Jules's couch the day before the funeral. I needed help sorting out this wonky combination of deep sadness and profound hope. I paid good money for the therapists and coaches in my life to help me slow down and appreciate the moment and to remind me to breathe. And that's exactly what Jules told me to do first.

"Breathe and sit in it."

I did as I was told, and I swear I could feel the power of life and death with each breath. The yin and the yang, the crazy volts of energy that were continuously flowing. She talked me through it, explaining that the feelings I had weren't exclusive of each other; they worked together. Life might have ended for my Paw Paw, but I had faith that he was in a better place and happy as a clam to be sitting right next to Mee Maw, holding her hand. And on top of that, my professional life as I'd known it was ending, but I had faith that my work family would always love me and cheer me on as I created my dream career.

I believed all these things and was honored to share a few of these sentiments the very next day at the funeral. I got up in front of a church full of family and friends who all loved Paw Paw and started what I hoped would feel like a conversation with a friend.

"Am I the only one whose ever heard and believed that bad things happen in threes?"

Several in the room smiled and nodded letting me know I wasn't the only one.

"Well, when I heard about Paw Paw passing away, I started trying to quickly look for two other things so I could tick them off and feel better knowing all the bad stuff was over. Such a strange superstition, but it got me to thinking: What if we were able to shift our mindset from the negative way of thinking about these three seemingly 'bad things' and instead found a way to believe that they are, in fact, beautiful and joyful new beginnings? Instead of focusing on the loss, we have the choice to focus on the hope that rises when something is lost or must be left behind. If we can choose hope, we could look out and dream of what amazing thing is to come in our lives, even in the midst of an ending! That might not be an easy task, but I want to challenge myself and you to try and look for the joy and hope that can come from endings. Paw Paw might have left us here, but he got to join Mee Maw in heaven, and that brings me so much joy thinking of them reunited."

I paused before sharing the other thing I felt I'd learned in this process: the gift of legacy.

"When I think of legacy, I think of the essence of someone that comes to mind when you hear that person's
name. To understand and appreciate legacy, you have
to have experienced that person, spent time with them,
and watched their life in motion to know exactly what
they are leaving behind."

As I looked out at the crowd in the room, I decided to share
the three things that I saw as Paw Paw's legacies, knowing that
just by sharing them, I'd solidify them in my heart and soul as
guiding lights in my own future.

"First is his kindness—his genuine happiness to see
me, my cousins, and our families. He would give you
these big, awkward bouncy hugs, and you just knew he
was glad you were there. His second legacy is of course
fishing."

So many people in the room smiled and looked to their
neighbor in agreement. Paw Paw loved to fish and be near the
water. It was a part of his life, which made it part of our childhood. Mee Maw and Paw Paw lived near a lake after building
their retirement home and being on a boat with him brought
back fond memories. It was a part of who he was and how people experienced him in life.

"And last but not least, Paw Paw is leaving behind a
legacy of being a man who showed up."

I didn't have the best words to express exactly what I meant, and "showed up" didn't even sound like proper English to me. But still, it seemed to fit just right.

"Paw Paw showed up for his country, joining the Navy and serving in both WWII and the Korean War. He'd shown up as a businessman, creating his family owned electric business that his children still own and operate. He was the one who took me to get my driver's permit. He built me a nightstand for my childhood bedroom that I still have and a bookshelf for my sister for her classroom during her first year of teaching. He was at graduations, at weddings, at hospitals when grand- and great-grandbabies were born, at Veteran's Day events at school with his great-grandchildren. He was there. He showed up and was there for the people in his life."

But the thing I wanted to share about legacies was the beautiful way they were handed down from one generation to the next. How could I know that Paw Paw had left these legacies behind?

"I'll tell you how I know. I've already seen his legacy in action in my very own children, his great-grandchildren."

With tears in my eyes and after a few pauses to catch my shaky voice, I told them how I'd shared with both of my children separately that Paw Paw had passed away. When I told

Elizabeth, my beautiful, blue eyed daughter, her very first reaction was to ask me, "What about Grandpa? How is Grandpa?"

Grandpa was my dad, the man who had lost his dad and had become his roommate after the divorce with my mom.

"Is he going to be okay?"

Her reflex response to dive into her tender, caring heart and think of someone else? Well, it assured me that Paw Paw's legacy of caring kindness would live on through her.

When I told my son Trace, who was a country boy who loved hunting and fishing through and through, he said, "Paw Paw made these lures by hand, and I didn't ever get to go and do that with him. Do you think there's any way that I could inherit some of those lures?"

I was grinning cheek to cheek and said, "Of course. I'll talk to Grandpa and see if you can inherit some of those."

It wasn't only Paw Paw's love of fishing that I could see flowing down to Trace; it was also the appreciation for what some would see as small things. The fact that he wanted something to remember him by—an inheritance that had nothing to do with money or a bank account, but a piece of something Paw Paw had created—*that* was the legacy. Paw Paw hadn't been a rich man or one of endless means, but he'd worked hard, provided for his family, and found joy in simple outdoor pleasures.

The last legacy that I had already seen taking hold in the next generation was Paw Paw's ability to show up, and I saw it in no one other than myself. I shared my very own story of struggling to go and visit him in the hospital just weeks before.

Since he was in a hospital just miles from my home, I knew

I should go and see him once I'd gotten word that he was out of surgery and in stable condition. It scared me though. Hospitals were scary to me. I hadn't been back at a hospital to visit anyone facing a dire situation since JoAnn. I knew that Paw Paw was fragile, and I didn't know if I could bear looking at his mortality knowing that I would also be reminded of my very own.

I wavered on going to see him but kept feeling the pull to go. I told myself I was going there to support my dad, but on the day that I finally got up my courage to stop by, I found that my dad wasn't there. When I walked down to Paw Paw's room, he was sleeping, and he didn't look like himself. He had always been such a lively man with a warm smile, and now for the first time, he looked fragile and unwell.

I panicked. I walked out and texted my dad, asking if he was coming back and looking for a lifeline. I was the one needing support.

"What should I do?" I asked him.

"I won't be back for a while. Leave if you need to or go in and see if you can wake him."

Ugh. The decision was mine to make, and I was still scared.

I hadn't been this close to death since JoAnn. While no one had said Paw Paw could go at any minute, I knew things didn't look great, and I didn't know if I was up for the emotional exposure that waking him in this state might bring. Irrational as it might seem, I had a hidden fear that he wouldn't wake up at all or, if he did, that something would go wrong. I was afraid that I'd be there to witness his final moments. To see someone's last breath firsthand.

I paced back and forth down the long hallway, deciding if I'd head back to his room to face my fears or straight to the elevator that would take me down to ground level to my car. Back and forth down the hallway I went until I finally had enough guts to walk back over to his room. I peeked in, and he was still sleeping. I couldn't decide what to do.

There was a young nurse at a computer station right outside his room. She had her head down, focused on her work. I decided maybe this young lady could help me, so I interrupted her and said, "Look, he's sleeping. Should I wake him up, or should I just go? I should probably just go, right? Or what do you think?"

She smiled. And I think right then God decided to speak straight through her to tell me these words: "Girl, he has been snoring all day. You can totally wake him up."

Really? Okay, so just wake up the snoring 90-year-old?

I had to laugh because she made it sound like such an easy thing to do. I decided to take her advice though. I could do this. I walked in slowly and reached down to hold his hand. He woke up, and instantly, I was reminded that he had the most sparkly blue eyes. I couldn't remember the last time that I ever really looked at Paw Paw in the eyes. Wow, they were blue.

I didn't know what to say, and I could tell he was tired. I didn't know where to start, but then I remembered something I'd seen my mom do. I grabbed my phone and showed him a picture that I'd found the night before of him and Mee Maw with Trace. Trace was a baby, and when I showed it to him, he instantly lit up.

"That's Trace!"

I teared up at that moment and probably will always tear up when I think of it because that was Paw Paw, a man who genuinely seemed so happy to see you or anyone else as soon as you walked into a room. He greeted that picture with a smile, just like he would have had Trace been standing right next to him. We talked a little bit more, but he started to doze off. It was time to go, but first, I had to let him know that I loved him.

I looked him in the eyes and said, "I love you, Paw Paw."

I left feeling proud to have walked into that room, proud to have looked him in the eyes, and proud to be his granddaughter. I was proud that I had made a choice to go and be with him, just like he would have done for me. I was proud that I'd woken up a 90-year-old man who'd been snoring all day. I was proud that I'd shown up.

And then I shared with the people in the room one of my final memories—something that happened as Paw Paw and I were saying our goodbyes that day. He looked me in the eyes and said, "Thank you for coming."

"Of course, Paw Paw. You're welcome. I'm glad that I came."

I told the people in the room that I hadn't been able to stop thinking about what he'd said.

Thank you for coming.

"At first glance, it seemed like a polite thing that anyone might say, but then I realized that I'd heard it before. Not even a year back, Mee Maw, Paw Paw's wife of over

65 years, had said the exact same thing when I visited her at the nursing home just months before she passed."

Thank you for coming.

I'd come to believe that it wasn't just something nice they said to people, even though I believe in their Southern hospitality. It was more than that. It was two people from a generation that did not typically speak words of love or strong emotion reaching out from a deep, soul level to express their sincere gratitude when people showed up for them.

Thank you for coming.

It was Paw Paw's and Mee Maw's final legacy handed down to me, and it would forever mean so much more than a gracious goodbye.

"Don't you see? Thank you for coming means so much more. It means thank you for caring about me. Thank you for looking me in the eye. Thank you for giving me your time. Thank you for proving that I matter to you. Thank you for showing up. I am thankful for Paw Paw and the beautiful legacies he has passed down, and I thank you all for showing up to honor him today."

Back at home that afternoon, I did a final review on my farewell email. On top of preparing for my funeral remarks, I'd been drafting the firm-wide email to let everyone know that I'd be leaving. The message to the masses was yet another struggle for me to find the exact words to convey my gratitude for the people who would click the email open.

For some people, putting in their notice or sending a final, "Peace out," email would be no big deal, but it was different for me. Leaving a place where the people and culture felt etched in my heart was not going to be easy. Over the years, I had been supported and cared for during good times and bad and had the most fun with the most amazingly kind people. These people had high fived me in the halls, dance partied me out of funks, brought my children and me gifts when we were happy, sad, or hurt.

I was leaving my work family, and I'd been mourning the loss slowly since my first conversation with the managing partner. Now that it was time to share with everyone, a big ol' dose of reality was hitting me square in the heart.

Oh my goodness, I am actually going to do this! I am going to tell everyone, and this is really going to happen.

Hitting send would not only be a sad goodbye, but it would be one step closer to me actually leaving and heading out into the unknown.

But it was Paw Paw's words that swirled in my mind as I finally had the heart to click send.

Thank you for coming.

At 4pm on that Thursday, just hours after I had spoken at Paw Paw's funeral and listened to a uniformed Navy sailor play

"Taps" on his trumpet at the graveside service, the time had come. The email was sent, and my work family now knew that I'd be leaving.

The email was gone, but I was left with a sense of peace. What a week! It had been an intense week of loss. But just as I'd shared with folks that morning, I had a choice. I could latch onto the sadness, the exhaustion, and overwhelm that I'd been feeling. Or I could open my mind and embrace the beautiful hope for things to come. All I had the energy to do was pray that I would honor the legacies given me by my family of origin and my work family. I prayed that I would show up for the people in my life and thank them for coming into mine.

Chapter 12

Signs Along the Road

"WHY WOULDN'T YOU GO?"

JP looked at me with what seemed like genuine curiosity and surprise. He'd asked me this question just days before Paw Paw's funeral that was scheduled for a Thursday morning. Months before I had decided to sign up for a retreat that Michelle Chalfant was hosting in Nashville. Michelle was an author, therapist, and host of a podcast called *The Adult Chair*. A friend had told me about her, and I'd grown to appreciate her work. Signing up for the retreat was something completely new for me.

I'd never been to anything like it. I was going to have to travel, meet new people, and try to stay totally open to whatever was planned during the *Finding Self-Love and Living Authentically* retreat. I was nervous about it, but I'd finally decided months back that it was worth the risk. I'd signed up, booked flights, and even chose to get a single room on campus where the workshop would be held.

Only thing now was that I was supposed to fly out first thing Friday morning. After the emotional rollercoaster that this week had been, I didn't know if I could do it. I was spent. I didn't know if I was strong enough to tackle what I was sure would be an emotional journey over the weekend. I debated internally and even emailed to ask if I'd get my money back if I bailed out.

But when I mentioned not going to JP, his quick response threw me. The tone and spirit of his question spurred me to ask myself the same thing.

Why wouldn't you go, Dena?

And the internal dialogue continued.

Maybe, just maybe, you can handle it. Maybe, just maybe, you are strong enough to keep going. Remember, you are capable of more!

After the mental chatter subsided, I decided then and there: I'd go. I didn't know how I'd feel, how I'd deal, or if this was a horrible time to walk into something so new. But still, I'd go. I would show up. And showing up meant I had to drag myself and my vulnerability all the way to Nashville the morning after the funeral and my farewell email.

The alarm went off before 5 am that Friday morning, and as I made myself get out of bed and off to the airport, I wondered what the heck I was doing. I was so tired. I was not feeling the energy, the love, or any level of enthusiasm. I felt like crap. All I could think to do was pray.

God, help me. God, help the women I'll meet at this workshop. Help us be brave and charge into the uncertainty, risk, and emotional exposure this weekend might bring. God, help me figure out what self-love is all about. Help me make it through the weekend, but more importantly, God, please just help me find a place to take a nap. Thanks, God. Amen.

When I landed in Nashville, I headed straight to the Scarritt Bennett Center where the workshop would be held and where my hopeful heart prayed that my room would be ready. I arrived well before the posted check-in time, and even though I said at least one million prayers and affirmations and had my fingers and toes crossed that there was an empty room, I was told I'd have to wait.

A couple of hours later, I was ecstatic when I got word that my room was ready. I walked across the small campus to the dorm. I put the key into the door and found a tiny room with a twin bed, dresser, mirror, and a stand for my suitcase. It was no frills, no fuss, definitely not a, "We fancy!" type room. But for me, it was perfect. After working my way through a highly emotional week, a stripped-down room with only the necessities felt oddly comforting.

I closed the blinds, turned up the AC, and crawled into the not-so-soft twin bed. And I slept. Hard. I woke up several hours later and took a quick shower. Then, I was ready. I walked slowly toward the retreat meeting room. While my dorm room might have been plain, the campus was gorgeous. I'd missed it while in my sleepy stupor earlier in the day. It was right next to Vanderbilt University and nestled under a cascading green canopy of trees. Something about it felt special.

After walking by a few buildings and a garden with a labyrinth, I found the spot. I slowly climbed up the single flight of stairs and saw a large room at the end of the hall. Following a few signs letting me know I was on the right track, I found myself in a large room that felt more like a parlor. (Confession: I don't think I've ever actually been in a parlor, but this seemed like the kind of room you'd call a parlor.)

I took stock of the situation. The room was carpeted with tables and chairs, stained glass windows, high ceilings, sofas and armchairs tucked into niches, and dark wooden bookshelves lining the walls. But more than the furniture, I was curious about the people in the room. I counted. There were eleven women total.

We were asked to take a seat, and, after a round of introductions, everyone seemed normal. I might have looked brave on the surface, but inside, I was scoping out my situation and felt confident the other women were, too. I wondered if they were asking themselves the questions I was asking myself.

Why is she here?

What's her story?

What is she looking for from all of this?

Michelle was the leader. She felt like an acquaintance since I'd been listening to her podcast for awhile at that point. I knew her voice, but now I got to see her in action. She was excited to share with us all she had planned on finding self-love and living authentically. She had an energy about her that was warm and welcoming.

During the first few hours that made up Day 1, I got to meet all of the ladies and dive into a few of their stories. It was fascinating. So many different ages, situations, vocations, but still, very similar desires. We wanted to find our voices. We had dreams but didn't know how to get started on them. We wanted to regain power and control of our own lives. We wanted to love ourselves and feel confident.

We'd each had different childhoods, adolescent years, and now adult lives, but we were more the same at the core than we were different. And I found that to be the most interesting to me. Not that I wasn't enjoying the personal activities. I was. I mean, how often do you find yourself lying on the ground doing a guided meditation where you imagine yourself flying around on a magic carpet? Not too often.

But while I stayed focused and did my work, I couldn't help but be aware of the fact that I was not alone. There were ten other women doing their own work all around me. I was fascinated that while I so often found myself feeling alone at home, there were women from all over who felt exactly like me. They had even sought out a cool new experience of a group retreat, too!

We were strangers, but I kept being reminded when I saw another woman in the room sharing in the experience that we really knew each other's stories at some level. While the specifics of some of the hardships or victories we'd faced might have been different, one part of our stories was the same. We all wanted hope, and connection, and love.

After a full afternoon and evening of the first third of Michelle's program, we gathered over a meal before calling it a day. Traveling and the emotional work involved in opening myself up to something new yet again had worn me out. I was proud of myself as I got in bed that first night. I had shown up.

After a great night's sleep, I woke up hungry. My soul had been fed with the previous day's session, but now it was time to feed my belly. I had a couple of hours to kill before we started, so I took a walk to the local Starbucks.

When I made it back to campus, I still had time to explore. I walked slowly as the sun came shining through the trees on campus. I stopped and stared up at the brick arches where words like, "The World is My Parish," looked back at me. I chased the sun around campus, taking pictures on my iPhone when I came upon a breezeway flanked by two stone archways. On one side it read: "Expect Great Things From God."

What a morning message! I was now only months away from leaving the corporate world and heading into self-employment. It was a great reminder that I had to continually hold to my faith, believing that great things could and would happen. I stood there thinking for several moments enjoying the gift of not being in a rush. I needed to remember the rewards of pumping the breaks on the usual fast pace of life. When I allowed myself to slow down, I kept receiving these moments of calm and clarity.

As I walked through the breezeway and looked back at

where I'd come from, I saw the opposite archway. The words, "Attempt Great Things For God," stared back at me. I stood there frozen, hot chai in my hand. I kept reading it over and over. Unlike the other side, which seemed like a gentle reminder, these words sounded more like a command. It was a, "You better do what I'm saying right here," kind of thing.

Those words—"Attempt Great Things For God"—had been etched into stone and were now burning into my mind a reminder. A reminder that I wasn't only supposed to hold to my hope of things to come in joyful expectation; I was supposed to act out of faith with willful intention. Action would be required, not only in my future professional endeavors but in all parts of my life.

A deep sense of gratitude came over me for what I considered to be signs meant to guide me along my journey. These words etched in stone were bread crumbs that I know God, the Universe, and probably JoAnn left for me to find. Sure, they were there for anyone to see, but I believed that they were also there for me to find in this exact moment to encourage me. This archway wasn't the first time I had seen and felt something like this, and I believed it wouldn't be the last sign I welcomed into my journey.

The signs were different than the voices I'd heard in my mind. The internal whispers from my intuition or calls straight from my gut to my heart always led me to explore something deeper I was facing in my life. And choosing to explore what the voices had to say always led me to learn new things or try out new perspectives, but it also wore me out. So, I decided to believe that the signs I saw were things that I needed to help me stay the course that I had chosen to follow.

Basically, I needed a pick me up! A little, *"We see you!"* from the Universe to give me a gentle, loving reminder that I wasn't alone. I needed some assurance that all was well. I was slowly learning what I'd need to keep myself moving forward because I was just like any other human. I would lose my energy, get discouraged, and allow doubt to creep in. But it always seemed that in those moments, a sign would appear.

I couldn't keep staring at the sign I'd found that morning because I had a full day of workshop ahead of me. I got myself ready and made it back to the room where the strangers, who now felt like acquaintances and maybe almost friends, were waiting. We greeted each other with smiles and went through a full day of individual and group exercises.

As we wound and balanced our way through time alone and in groups, many times sharing bits of our personal journeys, I was continuously comforted by the fact that I was not alone. It continued to strike me and make me smile. While I had my own personal journey, there were similar stirrings that many of us shared. I found each woman said some specific thing that would hit me just as I must have needed it to.

That's the power of women convening and sharing their real-life stuff. We get so wrapped up in our own minds that we convince ourselves that we're the only ones dealing with x, y, or z. But we aren't alone in this thing called life. And when we come together and share our realities from a place of nonjudgmental kindness, there is massive power to be found. I felt connected to the other women and was reminded of the renewing effect that community and authenticity has on the heart and soul.

After another full day of the workshop and an amazing Thai dinner shared with a smaller group of the women, my heart, soul, and belly were full. I slept and woke the following morning ready to see what the final day of the retreat had in store. But before the workshop, I met two of the women at a local coffee shop for breakfast. It was a cute place with things like, "Choose Love," and, "You Are Magic," written on the water dispensers. I sat down with the number 5 marker that I'd been given by the server to put at my table while I waited for my food. As I walked to the table, I was smiling and told the ladies, "And another 5. All the time, that's all I see now."

I told them all about the signs that kept popping into my life. I told them about the one from the day before and how the signs weren't always as big as rock archways like I'd seen on campus.

"One of the little signs that has become a mainstay in my life is the number five. I see 5:55 on the clock all the time. I'll drive by and see a 555 address, get a 5 at a restaurant like this one. Five, five, five. I finally started taking screenshots of them and told JP there was something up with this 5-thing."

One of my fellow self-love retreaters said, "Have you heard of angel numbers? You should look it up."

I hadn't, and neither had one of the other girls, so we quickly grabbed our phones and searched it up. I read and started laughing.

Based on the website we found, the angel number 555 was

said to carry strong vibrations of making decisions and life choices, personal freedom and individuality, life lessons learned through experience, new opportunities, adventure, curiosity, challenges, action, and activity. Angel number 555 was said to tell of significant and necessary changes happening in your life that had been divinely inspired and guided. These changes were supposed to bring about long-awaited circumstances and results that would fully align me with my true divine life purpose and soul mission.

What the?!

The website we checked out even said that my angels were telling me to let go of old patterns that weren't serving me positively and to trust that better things would replace them. It said to know that my angels were always with me, asking me to "Go with the flow."

Wow.

Some might think that it was all goofy, new-agey, woo-woo stuff, but I decided that my God—the one I was buds with—well, He liked to have some fun. There was no harm in believing that God told the angels to figure out fun ways to try and guide us on our paths. Others could decide for themselves if they wanted to believe it, but I was in.

I didn't go off and do anything differently with this newfound 555 information. I just decided to appreciate the messages I believed I was getting and take them as confirmation that I would, in fact, be just fine. That's all I wanted. I wanted to know that at the end of the day—at the end of all this change—I was going to be okay. All would be well.

JP brushed my sign sightings off when I started telling him about them, saying I was just more aware now but that the fives had always been there. I got that. But I didn't really care. The point was, not only was I aware of a few repeating signs, but I was also conscious to their presence in my life. I went ahead and welcomed them with an open mind. It was a win for the freedom I was searching for and that so many others were, too. We wanted to be confident and believe what we believed, even if not everyone agreed with us.

I had welcomed the signs and kept an open mind, not just over the last few months but the last three days as well. I'd made it to the last afternoon of the workshop, and it was time to join the graduating class of the self-love and authentic living workshop weekend! I wasn't graduating in a sense that I could look you in the eye and say with confidence, "I love myself and will forever live authentically!"

Nah, that wasn't where I was yet.

But I could tell I was oh so close. I had moments when I could feel my inner confidence coursing through my veins. Not fake, outer confidence, but an internal kind that hummed and buzzed with a new mantra.

You are safe. You matter. You are capable. You are worthy. You got this!

Still, those moments would fade, and other nagging voices would return. Then, I'd have to feel, deal and heal all over again. And I was starting to wonder if maybe that's as far as I'd ever get. Maybe I'd always have to reach into all the parts of me and ask what they needed. Maybe I'd always have to slow down and look for signs to keep me on course. I could deal with that. I was starting to be okay with whatever worked for me.

And maybe that's what unconditional self-love is really all about. Maybe it's cutting myself some slack, giving myself an, "Atta girl!" when I need it, and forgiving myself when I jack it all up. Maybe it's granting myself the grace that I pray I give to others. Maybe I'm further along on the road to loving myself than I thought I was.

At the time, I didn't know for sure. But what I also didn't know was that God had more signs to give me before I headed out and back to the real world.

Michelle asked every woman to come up to grab a hug and a little memento to take home. Inside little gift bags were hand-crafted ceramic hearts with a word written on the back. Michelle said each heart had a different word that would find the exact woman it needed to go home with. As I walked up, I was excited.

What would my heart say?

I grabbed my hug and my gift bag and went to sit back down. I unwrapped it slowly and turned it over in my hand.

Witness.

That was the word written in black ink. It might not have made sense to some, but it made perfect sense to me. Growing up I had been taught how to witness to others. What I'd been taught as a child was to share the good news of Jesus. I hadn't "witnessed" in that way in years, but I was quickly reminded that my newly uncovered life mission was to share my story and inspire others toward their dreams with words. That's what a witness is—someone with knowledge of an event or change from personal observation or experience. And I had knowledge of personal growth and development and reigniting dreams because I was living it!

I get it, God. You want me to be a witness.

With my ceramic heart packed safely in my bag, I waited on the curb for my ride to the airport. I turned to look at the campus again and admired the Wightman Chapel behind me. I tried to take a quick peek inside, but the doors were locked. Instead, I found a historical marker and read it while I waited. When I got to the middle of the plaque, I was hit with yet another beautiful sign.

None other than Martin Luther King, Jr. had preached at that very chapel some 60 years before. I was standing on holy ground.

God, it was fun. It was fun to feel connected to the past, to the present, and to the future—all linked by dreams and people who felt called to witness. I could feel the love, and I hopped into the car knowing that I was going to be okay. I trusted in that fact. I just had to keep following the signs.

Chapter 13

Life Goes On

"WILL WE LOSE THE HOUSE?"

That was my daughter's first and only question when I told her that I'd be leaving my job. I guess the need for security runs in our DNA. I sat in stunned silence for a second before throwing out the answers that bubbled into my mind.

"Of course not . . . Well, I don't think so . . . No, we shouldn't."

Her question made me sad, but I was ready to talk her through this apparent fear. I told her that her Dad and I had made the decision and felt confident that we could continue to live in our home. We might have to modify some of our habits and be more mindful of our spending, but we could make smart choices with our money until I got my business up and running.

It was early October, and with four months and counting until my last day, it felt like we were in the homestretch but still with time to plan. Even as I'd planned for this conversation, I never expected that my news would have her mind go from 0 to 100 in seconds. I had already asked myself and JP these same questions.

What if my business doesn't succeed?

What if I don't make any money?

What if we can't afford the house?

We had savings, and we had time. We'd figured it out as part of our decision-making process.

Trace listened to his sister's questions and listened to me confirm that we were safe. I told her I would even show her each month when I sent in the mortgage payment—whatever it took to keep that concern out of her mind. But when it was Trace's turn to ask questions, he went straight to business.

He looked me straight in the eyes and said semi-mockingly, "Well, you better get to writing your book, huh?"

My mind ran through the response I wanted to say.

Yes, punk, I have work to do, you twelve-year-old practical, Mr. Fix It, man-child.

However, my semi-calm parental voice stepped in to assure him that I would put in the work to try and make my business a success. They hadn't known mommy as anything other than someone who worked downtown at a cool building. They understood Daddy was his own boss, even though I don't think they understood the inherent risk in his businesses. But it appeared that they realized that my change would have an impact on their lives. They'd both gone in two different directions with the news; One to the need for security, and the other to action. I loved seeing myself in both of their reactions.

And honestly, I still felt pulled in opposite directions. I was trying to keep things moving forward on my new venture, but with a foot still in my old job, I felt torn and unable to enjoy either. Luckily, it was time for what had become my annual trip to visit JoAnn. After the prior year's emotional release, I decided I needed to make it a regular thing. So on October 15, 2017, I sat and rested by JoAnn's side. I never had a plan when I came to visit. It was a quiet space to just be. When I was about to leave after some quality time, I closed my eyes, took a deep breath, and waited. It didn't take long to hear the whisper clear as day.

Keep going. Just keep going.

I took it in for a moment. *Alright then, I hear you. But keep going where? How far, how fast, and for how long?*

I only had a few months left now, and I wanted to enjoy it. I wanted to love on the people I was working with and not feel torn or divided. Then, I remembered something JoAnn used to always say: Simplify.

I wondered if I could keep going and simplify my life at the same time. I decided it was worth a shot. I would simplify. I would let Dena Speaks wait for me just down the road while I took in all the final sights and sounds of corporate life. I would honor both my current and future careers by intentionally slowing down and giving myself permission to soak in the last days of this phase of my life.

From that day on, I went in to the office every day and tried to connect with anyone I could. I shared coffees, lunches, dinners, hugs, and impromptu dance parties with my coworkers and clients. They might not need me much longer, but I needed them and the memories I was still creating. I slowed down and savored every day.

My time at the firm wasn't the only thing winding down. As October turned into December, so was the year that had been 2017. My year of Balanced Freedom. What a booger it had been. I'd come to believe that once I survived a year, I earned a non-existent badge to put on my non-existent sash. My daughter's Girl Scout troop inspired me. When I saw girls with vests and sashes full of patches showing all they'd learned and conquered, I wanted something just like it.

My sash only had one badge for the year of Fearless Growth—my first daring journey into my fears and personal growth. And I was so close to earning my Balanced Freedom badge. I'd honed in on me, myself, and I, but I'd also become closer to my family and a short list of dear friends.

So, on a cool night in December while the boys were off hunting, I built another fire at the campsite. With a gorgeous sunset off in the distance, I sat and wondered about 2018 and my next imaginary (yet completely necessary) badge. With the sound of the fire crackling and the heat warming my face and legs, my pulse slowed down. All was calm.

I was about to head into a period of my life that would be nothing but new roads, transitions at every corner, blind spots, and God knows what else. I would have to stay the course and remain calm. I closed my eyes and knew that was exactly what I'd need in the year to come.

I'd need calm.

I'd need to stay consistent.

I'd need calm and consistency.

Yes, that was it: Calm Consistency.

I got out my blank sheet of paper and pencil and drew some lines. What did I want for 2018? What did I wish for the year in front of me? Knowing where I was now, what did I want next? The list was shorter than previous years, more straightforward but still intentional.

I wanted connection.

I wanted a deeper personal relationship with God.

I wanted a deeper connection with JP, our kiddos, and my families—the one I was born into and the one I married into.

I wanted Dena Speaks to come to life.

In the middle of the page, I listed all the things I wanted to be sure I made happen, including deep breathing, deep feeling, deep connecting, big stepping, large living, strong hugging, kind sharing, risk taking, and gut laughing.

I wrote: "It's gonna be a heck of a year!"

The heart in the far-right corner said Meant for More and was surrounded by the badges that had come before: Fearless Growth and Balanced Freedom. And I'd picked my 2018 battle cry:

Calm Consistency.

With my new mantra top of mind, I eased into 2018 ready to embrace all there was left at the office, knowing that I'd enter all the new doors ahead of me in due time. I wrapped up my final client work in January, attaching my signature to my last audit reports. Then we celebrated at a farewell party, planned with love by team members that knew all the things I loved: good friends, good food, and a great romantic comedy movie! The marquee at the venue read, "Goodbye ML&R, Hello Dena Speaks." They gave me a wooden sign filled with nothing other than words of inspiration as a beautiful token of love and appreciation.

My partner in crime, Sara, said a few parting words, and I tried to do the same without crying too much. Then I sat in a private theater surrounded by people that I loved, and we watched *Notting Hill*. We laughed and cried when Julia Roberts reminded Hugh Grant that she was just a girl, standing in front of a boy, asking him to love her. I mean come on, how could there not have been a few misty eyes as we walked out of the theater?

What I didn't expect, though, was that I'd have those same misty eyes days later on my official last day. I'd been mourning this loss for months, if not years now, so I thought I might be a little more prepared to face a door that would soon be officially closed to me. Sure, I thought I might cry, but I hadn't expected the tears to be triggered by a silly little thing like my badge.

I'd had a dream just a few days earlier that I was running around frantically asking, "Where the heck is my badge? I hate it when I forget my badge. I can't get in the door. I have to walk all the way around to the other entrance. Ugh."

For 15 years, I had a glossy badge with my picture and name

on it. It was even on one of those fun, clip-on retractable things. I was a woman with a badge. But as I was preparing to walk away from corporate life and my work family on my last day, I was asked to turn in my badge. Twice.

The first time, I smiled kindly and assured them I wouldn't forget. But the second time, I held it close and sped the opposite direction. I ran to the office that I shared with my co-worker, Lesley, and the tears started to fall hard.

I didn't think I could part with it. I wanted to take it with me, to hold on to it. Not to sneak back in the office, but because for some reason, that dang badge had come to mean more than just a beep at the door. The badge made sense. It gave me access. It told people who I was and that I had a right to be in the place I was in.

Where I was going next, there was no door for me to access, no office to enter, no people waiting. And honestly, it was weird. That badge had been a part of the consistency that had been my professional life, and now I had to give it back. It was time to trade in that badge for the hope of earning new ones. Badges to go alongside Fearless Growth, Balanced Freedom, Calm Consistency, and other mantras my future would hold.

I was prepared to turn in my badge, but I chickened out and couldn't test the limits of my vulnerability. I'm a rule follower, so I left it with Lesley and told her she'd have to do it for me. I couldn't willingly hand it over myself. That dang badge had secured my place in a space with other people and had given me a sense of belonging—belonging to a team of people in a building where we got great work done.

I hadn't thought of it like that all the years I'd tucked it in my pocket or thrown it in my purse. But now that I wouldn't have it, I wasn't sure where I belonged. Was it just me, myself, and I now? I already felt lonely. But I had to keep going. I had to remain calm and consistently put one foot in front of the other. Left, right. Left, right.

And that's what I did after hugging a few last necks and saying my last goodbyes. Trying to look as cool and calm as I could, I walked out the door with a lump in my throat and went straight to my car.

I sat there knowing my life was going to be different. I put on my sunglasses, turned on the car, and headed out of the parking garage. I'd driven away before knowing there was a two-month break ahead of me, but this was more than a sabbatical. It was a real departure.

And oddly and wonderfully, I had peace about it. Life would go on.

Sure enough, it did. The sun set that night, and it came back up the next day, and the next, and the next. The world had not stopped moving because I had changed my circumstances. The firm opened its doors Monday, and my children went to school. I was at home and didn't have a job to get to, but I still mattered. I still had worth. Life just looked and felt different now.

It was a gentle reminder that life was a crazy, beautiful journey, and I was merely a part of it.

Chapter 14

I Have a Dream

"EVERYBODY HAS A VOICE. Don't be afraid to stand up for yourself. Treat others the way you want to be treated. As she travels around to different places to teach other people to be brave like she is, she is still trying to teach me to be brave here at home. So everybody welcome, my mom, the bravest woman I know, Dena Jansen."

It was the night of February 22, 2018. I sat in my seat of the movie theater I'd rented out for my Dena Speaks private launch party with family and friends. My expectant nerves were almost overtaken by the pride I felt for my daughter. I could barely believe what I'd just heard. Her introduction was beautiful.

What people didn't know what that less than 60 minutes before, Elizabeth had gotten nervous. She was so scared, she didn't know if she could introduce me and share the welcome she'd written. My little girl found herself with a choice to make—one that so many of us have had to make. Would she allow fear to hold her back?

Of course, I wouldn't force her to do it. But I would use it as an opportunity to remind her that she had a choice to make for herself. She ducked her head and listened as we talked through the options. She could go up and do the introduction all by herself like we'd planned. She could have my sister, Mandy, read her words for her while she stood alongside. Or maybe, they could stand together, and Mandy could read until she was comfortable and ready to shine.

She thought it over. We assured her that any choice she made was going to be the right one. This was an opportunity to work through her fear and be brave, but it was also an opportunity to make her own decision. None of us would force her to do anything she wasn't comfortable with.

After some thought, she met herself in the middle and decided to share the introduction with her Aunt Mandy. They'd agreed on a spot where she'd take over near the end. But when their time arrived and Mandy read the words from the bright green piece of paper they'd printed it out on, Elizabeth actually chimed in a few lines earlier than they'd planned. She found her own brave voice and was ready to use it. It was beautifully coincidental that she jumped in with the words, "Everybody has a voice."

My precious, brave Elizabeth bounced up and down as she headed over to hand me the mic and give me a quick squeeze. I told her I loved her.

"Can I order a cookie now?"

I mean, it was her time to celebrate, too. So, of course I said yes! I got a hug from my sister as well, as they walked back to their seats, and I took my place in the spotlight. It was time to use my voice. But first, some part of me paused and thought back on how this dream of mine was now becoming my reality.

Months back, I'd decided there would be no better way to start my business than to have a party with my nearest and dearest family, friends, and colleagues. I wanted all the people in the different circles of my life in the same room, experiencing the same thing, with me. I wanted to share in a TED Talk style speech all I'd figured out about myself since my soul awakening and what I planned to do with myself and Dena Speaks. I wanted to create an evening full of connection, inspiration, and FUN!

I wanted everything about the night to mean something. I figured I'd need a few weeks to get my bearings after leaving so late February seemed reasonable. And it took me no time to request a date that would forever be my Dena Speaks anniversary. Thank goodness the theater was open that night, and I snatched it. February 22nd would be the day. It would be the day that I launched my dreams. And it was none other than JoAnn's birthday.

I put together an amazing Launch Team in Veronica, Chandler, and Sarah. Each would help make sure the night went off without a hitch. But on top of knowing I'd need help, I had to keep reminding myself *why* I was even doing it! The launch gave me another real-life opportunity to practice for myself all that I planned to preach—choosing bravery through your fears, exploring and learning new things, believing in my own purpose and potential, and sharing my journey with grace and authenticity.

And for months from the time I booked the venue to the morning of the event, I had planned. There would be a photographer and videographer, door prizes, and a movie at the end to allow all the people there some well-deserved down time. The fun was mapped out by the minute in the event timeline. I'd even made sure I was surrounded by love the entire morning of the event to make sure I didn't get any pre-launch jitters.

I was marrying myself and my dreams in front of a room full of loved ones that night, so it was the perfect reason to bring in my support reinforcements. Alisa and Janine flanked me as we started the morning with a flow yoga class. I trusted both of these women immensely. Both had given me strength before, and I felt stronger knowing they were by my side on the morning of the big launch. They were with me while I stood on my yoga mat trying to balance focus and anxiety.

The instructor walked through and introduced herself before class started. Before she could even ask my name, I blurted out, "It's a big day for me! I launch my business tonight, and I might puke."

"But you've got your girls here, just like bridesmaids."

And she was right. I had my girls. They would help usher me down the aisle. Everything would be alright. After some "ohms" and lots of deep breaths, Alisa and I went and met my mom for brunch. My mom was beside herself. She was excited for the night and threw out a toast for good luck as soon as our mimosas arrived. The yoga instructor's bridesmaids reference was starting to feel more like reality. It did, in fact, feel like a wedding day. We were all anxious and excited.

We loaded up the car with all the goodies. Inflatable microphones, Dena Speaks cups filled with Hershey kisses, one of my hot off the press business cards, and the picture frame and mat for all the guests to sign for me to keep as a memory of the night we'd share. We got to the theater, and just like that, the time had finally come.

The guests started to arrive. I hugged lots of necks, smiled until my cheeks hurt, and thanked so many dear people for coming. The theater was filled with people that I loved who were excited to see what was to come. They were smiling and talking, some meeting for the first time and others catching up with friends and family they'd known for years. All of my circles were merging just like I'd imagined.

Then at 6:28 pm, the lights went down, and the magic began. I wanted my children involved (and on camera) for my big night. So, Trace drew door prize winners alongside Chandler to ease into the night before passing the mic over to Mandy and Elizabeth. Even though I knew Elizabeth had experienced her very own pre-launch jitters, none of the people in the room would have known. After watching my daughter find and use her voice in the most inspiring way, it was my turn.

It was time for Dena to speak.

It would be hard to explain what this speech had come to mean to me. The speech was everything. Every word mattered.

I'd practiced countless hours in front of my bathroom mirror, holding an unplugged mic in my hand. It was my first public proclamation of who I now believed myself to be. It was twenty minutes of me baring my vulnerable soul in front of people that mattered.

These were friends and family members—families I'd been born into, married into, created myself, or had chosen to work with and for. I wanted to try and squeeze in every sweet ounce of gratitude I had in my short time with them, and I prayed they'd walk out feeling proud of me and proud of themselves and the roles they'd played in my life. I wanted them to be curious about what their own Meant for More journey could look like.

There was no more time for practice or prayers though; it was time to share my soul with my family.

As I stood there with a real mic in my hand and sixty plus real people staring back at me, I was ready. I was prepared. It was time to share about all the things that mattered to me.

"One of my heroes, Martin Luther King, Jr., once said, 'I have a . . .'?"

My smart and thankfully engaged friends and family called back, "DREAM!"

"Yes, I have a dream. He gave that speech over 55 years ago. But I remember hearing it for the first time back when I was in fourth grade. And I remember for the first time feeling the power of words. I was mesmerized.

And guess what? I have a dream, too. And sometimes dreams take time to mature, to become clearer and clearer. But if we give them the attention they deserve, they do become clearer. And as they become clearer, there comes a point where you either have to go for it and try to make them a reality or push them to the side."

I shared that just two years back, my life looked great from the outside looking in, but truth be told, I had been feeling more and more alone, isolated, and not as happy as I knew I could be. I just couldn't put my finger on what it was or how to fix it.

"I just wanted to fix it. But I couldn't. At least not until I hit some bumps in the road. Just like we all do in life. But some of those bumps felt to me like walls. Honestly, it felt like my life had fallen apart. And as I was wading through that difficult time in life, again, I remembered—even though I can't pin point the exact moment it happened—I realized that I had a choice. I could either choose to keep wading in this stuff, or I could choose hope."

Spoiler alert. I chose hope! And I told them as much.

"I decided if I chose hope, I would be able to piece my life back together in a way that I wanted to. But what I had to figure out then was what I wanted. Who was I? After some intense soul searching and relationship rebuilding, I figured out that what I wanted more than anything else was to feel free."

I took a deep breath and released it. *Calm consistency.*

"I wanted to feel like I had my arms out, wind blowing in my hair, sun in my face, eyes closed, (though hopefully not driving!). That was the free feeling I was searching for. I wanted the freedom I'd read about—the ability to stand alone but also have deeply connected relationships. I so desperately wanted to love who I was and stand on my own two feet. But I wanted to deeply connect with the ones who mattered the most to me—my family and my friends. The things that truly mattered way down deep. So once I figured that out, I decided I had to start my journey. My Meant for More journey—an intentional process of focusing on the things that mattered to me and building back up the life that I wanted."

I reminded them that as I started my journey, I quickly realized that I needed to know where the heck I was headed and who exactly had their hands on the wheel. So often in life, we put blinders on; we just start following whatever is in front of us, doing what we are "supposed to do." We don't stop to figure out who is in control.

But I decided I had to stop myself and do some soul searching. I had to ask myself questions. To figure out who I was and what I believed. Even though some of the answers that came back weren't always pretty, it was a necessary step in my process.

"And today, I would love to share with you a few of the things that I believe:
—I believe in the power of choice and the ability to change.
—I believe in the power of hope and the promise of potential.
—I believe in the power of dreams and the gifts of curiosity and creativity.
—I believe in laughter, fun, and impromptu dance parties.
—I believe that each one of us has the power to create and experience massive, positive change in our own lives and in relationships with others."

I paused to let it sink in.

"But actions speak louder than . . .?"

"WORDS!" My dear friends continued to play along with me, just like I hoped they would.

I shared that even though all of those words that I believed were beautiful, I had another choice to make. I had to decide if I was going to do anything about them. Would I work to make them a reality or push my dreams to the side again?

Spoiler alert: They all knew what I'd chosen obviously.

"So Dena Speaks is here! And I'm excited to launch this dream of mine to share my story and spark a light of curiosity in people. To get people dreaming again of the life they want to lead, the love they want to have, the corporate culture or career they want to build. That's what I want to get people excited about. My goal—my dream—is to create a community of true potential seekers. A community where regardless of our dreams—our very personal LIFE missions—that we share the same vision of creating stronger, happier, healthier versions of ourselves, our homes, our workplaces, and our communities."

The time and speech were flying by. It felt great to be sharing the real-life lessons I'd learned. I tried to be open, honest, and real about things that mattered to me. Personal growth may have sounded boring to some, but I was hoping they'd see it for what it really was: a strengthening of skills in bravery, courage, resilience, and creativity. All with the intention and ability to help us create the lives of our dreams.

"To make sure you are still with me. George Michael— anyone know that guy? He had a song, and it went something like: You gotta have . . .?"

I lingered in the question, but not long before the room eagerly chimed in with, "FAITH!"

"Heck yeah! We gotta have faith. If I didn't have faith, I wouldn't be here. Because without faith—without the ability to believe in things that you can't touch, or see, or feel—dreams would never come true."

A lump formed in my throat and tears sprung to my eyes, but I pushed through.

"So I'm going to hold tight to faith. Faith in myself. Faith in people like you—strong willed women and supportive dudes. And I am going to hold tight to my faith in a higher power that I will never be able to fully fathom, but I know has a plan for me and for you. Because you gotta have faith. So, let me ask you this quickly. Am I the only one who has ever had their faith shaken? Who has allowed fear, or disappointment, or anything else to get in the way of that faith? Am I alone?"

I wasn't. The murmurs of agreement confirmed it.

"Our faith will get shaken. But I am a firm believer that words matter. I'm a firm believer in the fact that our brains will believe what we tell it. So a couple months ago, I created what I call my Meant for More Mantra. These are the words that I tell myself, even when I am not believing or feeling them. This is my mantra."

Through a shaky voice I repeated it aloud to them.

"I am brave.

I have bold dreams.

I am full of confidence and conviction.

And I will continue to grow, day in and day out, not only because I am capable, but because I know in my heart and soul that I deserve all that life has to offer me! "

There it was. My Meant For More Mantra out there for the world to hear.

"You deserve the life of your dreams. You deserve those things because the people you surround yourself with believe that they matter. What you believe and what you actually do with your time matters. Your dreams matter! And the communities and people you invest in matter. But you're going to have to keep the faith because it's not going to be easy."

I told them to remember two things if they found themselves stuck in the everyday hustle and bustle of life, just like I had done and knew I would continue to on this journey.

"First, you always have a choice. The choice may not be a simple yes or no. It may not be an easy heads or tails flip of a coin. But you do have choices in your life, and you are in control of those choices. And two, whether those choices require you to make really big changes in your life or seemingly small changes, just remember that even small changes can add up to giant leaps of faith."

I invited them to get up on their feet so I could end with what I hoped would always be my parting words, regardless of where I was speaking, who I was speaking to, or what dreams the audience might be aspiring towards.

"Regardless of where your life takes you, where your dreams might have you go, whatever choices you make, please, just don't settle. Because whether you have the confidence and belief in yourself or not, please know, that I believe in you. Because you have believed in me. And I truly believe that every single one you and your hearts and souls are meant for more."

And then, it was time for me to ask them one last favor.

"So since this couldn't be awkward, would you all please cheer along with me? Not at me or for me, but *with me*, because you have all literally made my dreams come true!"

They played along perfectly as we all cheered and clapped. Tears of joy filled my eyes yet again. I'd had a dream, and it had come true. But it wasn't the time to cry. It was time to raise my arm, throw up a fist pump, and shout a little "Woo-hoo!" I tried with all my might to make the memory of the moments that had just passed permanent in my mind.

I went home that night thinking that I would crash and fall fast asleep, but instead, I was awake for hours. Reliving the entire night, feeling loved and supported. I had worked really hard. I had created an experience that would now be nothing more than a memory for many. And it had been worth every minute.

I had attempted a great thing.

I had surrounded myself with people who mattered to me and shared words that mattered with them. I had felt so many things all in the span of a few hours—fear, anxiety, calm, sadness, confidence, and ultimately, joy! And I had received some of the best compliments from several of my family and friends, and even more importantly, JP. They shared that they had teared up during my speech and felt truly inspired. That was one of the best feelings in the world—that I'd created a moment in someone's life that they'd remember!

But I needed more than just memories. So, I ordered a picture of the entire crowd to put behind the mat I now had filled with signatures and words of love and encouragement. I chose to print a picture the photographer took of the group being silly. It warmed my heart and made me smile. The photographer apologized that the print was so blurry. Many of the faces were not completely in focus. But I didn't care.

To me, it was perfect.

The picture was how I was finally choosing to see life—a little fuzzy sometimes, but always full of love, support, and fun!

When I look at that picture, I'll always be able to think back on the night where all of my dreams finally came into beautiful focus.

Chapter 15

Peace, Love and Comfort

DON'T RUSH ME.

The voice in my mind started as a whisper before it got louder and louder.

Don't rush me.

Do.
Not.
Rush.
Me.

I started hearing it just a few weeks after the launch party. I had taken off the day following the party to celebrate as best I knew how—over a meal with dear friends and a massage. But as days turned into weeks, I had a hard time coming off the high of the event and digging back down low into the details of launching a viable business.

I knew how businesses worked. I had audited them my entire career. I understood business cycles, but that didn't mean I enjoyed thinking on and creating my own. I knew full well what I *should* be doing. But I found it was easier to browse other speakers' websites, Instagram feeds, or Facebook pages and quickly be reminded of all they were doing that apparently was better than what I was doing.

I'd start and stop a project, get a little done, then dart back to make another list of all I had to, needed to, or should do. All I was doing well was spinning my wheels. Then, I'd hear the voice.

Don't rush me.

I slowed down and sat quietly one morning to try to hash it out.

What was the deal? Who or what was rushing me?

Answers came back slowly and over a few days, but the answers all pointed to the simple fact that I was doing what I had done for so long. I was struggling to prove that I mattered. That I had value. Still, after all this time, I was back where I started.

I had done such a brave thing. I'd left a career that offered me and my family financial security. I'd done what so many people never muster the courage to do. I left life as I'd known it to follow my heart. But here I sat just months into my new world, and I still felt lonely, scared, and uncertain of what I was doing and why.

For so many years, I had unconsciously tied my value to who I served and what I could produce. But now that I had no one to answer to—no clients to serve—all I had were blank pages leaving me feeling empty and alone. When these feelings set in, the cycle would continue as it had before. I'd allow comparison to take over and panic to set in, and I'd lose sight of what to do next. So many times, I'd choose to shut down.

This cycle of self-sabotage was much like a shame spiral where I would just walk down deeper and deeper into the dark. The shame spiral usually also came with a nice rush of heat, followed by sweat and a case of the nervous poos. It wasn't pretty. Jules drew a diagram months back trying to help me unpack these belief systems in my mind. It was messy. Circles and lines darted all over the whiteboard, but the one that stood out was the one that said this:

Replacement Belief: I matter. I have value.

That was a shift in perspective that I'd have to make. And I'd have to make it again and again it seemed. These replacement beliefs required that I go inward instead of out toward what other people thought or believed of me. I was being presented with another test—another chance to prove out my Meant for More concept. But what was the test? I sat on it for a few days and then I realized I knew the questions I had to answer for myself. I knew the choices I'd have to make.

Could I love myself enough to keep trying my best and grant myself grace if it didn't seem to measure up? Could I trust my own gut and intuition rather than give into what it appeared I *should* do? Could I feel all the feels instead of pretending that everything was fine? Could I ask for help as I moved forward instead of isolating myself? Could I keep putting myself out there, continuously living outside my comfort zone and pushing past my own limits and status quo?

Could I do all that?

Well, the easy answer was yes! Yes, I could. Because I already had been. I just might have to keep making the choice to keep doing it over and over again. And if I would stop trying to force myself to run, I believed that I could walk. I could chart my own course. Ecclesiastes 3 said there was a time for everything and a season for every activity under heaven. So it made sense that there would be a time for me to slow down and go at a pace that felt right to me. Then, there would be a time to keep moving forward.

With a sense of calm, I took a few deep breaths, imagining myself breathing in intention and exhaling expectation.

Breathe in intention—what do I want?

Breathe out expectation—what do others want or expect of me? Or what do I THINK they want or expect of me?

In the moment, I felt ready—ready to move on. But the Universe threw out another test my way to see if I was up for the challenge.

It was a warm and sunny afternoon in April 2018. I had set up a meeting with a woman who owned and operated a social media business. We'd met years back, but we'd run into each other recently and decided to catch up on both of our business ventures.

Under a giant oak tree on a beautiful day, we sat at an outside table of a co-working space in Austin. We talked for a good bit, me mostly answering questions that she was asking and her mostly taking notes—*pages* of notes.

"Should I be taking notes, too?" I asked her half-jokingly.

"No, this is just how I process things."

Ok, cool, then. But after the fourth page of notes, she started to explain to me how the social media landscape worked. She drew pictures and arrows, used words like platform, following, and algorithm to explain how her business helped launch or maintain an online presence for her clients.

I was trying so hard to keep up, but she got my full attention back when she shared the assessment of my readiness for her services. (I guess she'd been processing her thoughts in all those notes!)

"So maybe you aren't ready. It's taken me three pages of notes to know your why."

Oh brother, here we go again. Shame spiral here I come.

I knew what my "why" was all about. I had read and watched Simon Sinek's work, but I obviously wasn't articulating it clearly. I don't know if she realized I had tuned out and started down the spiral, but I had. Parts of me had their back turned, head down moving down, down, down. But other parts of me were defensive. Honestly, a feisty part of me was wagging her finger all hot and bothered.

Jeez, lady. I thought I was just answering your questions. You didn't ask me about my why until the third page of notes. Who do you think you are anyways? You don't think I'm ready? Well, maybe I'm not. Maybe I'll never be. But you don't get to tell me that.

After keeping my calm and composure, the meeting wrapped up and I headed home. But I couldn't shake the funk. I went to my neighbor Stefani, begging for company. She was kind and gracious and let me word vomit all over her. I told her about the evil social girl. Stefani did just what I needed her to do.

"I know, it's hard. The transition is hard. Finding your place in this new world will take time. But you will figure it out."

No coddling, no diving in and flaming the fires of self-doubt or fear, no trash talking. She just sat with me in my moment until she had to go home.

I wish she'd stayed because it might have kept me from eating three huge slices of pizza an hour later. Stefani's words had felt good, but comfort food tasted better. And that hot bread and cheese made me feel so much better . . . until it didn't. Not even an hour later, I was sick. I went to bed early, praying for it all to right itself by the next day.

I slept, and I woke up. And once I got to my journal and pen, I asked myself some questions.

What the heck is up? Why are you freaking out? Why do you feel so anxious?

And the answers didn't surprise me. Social media girl had triggered old patterns in me. I felt judged and found myself lacking. I don't think that was her intention in any way; it wasn't personal. But when what I was faced with externally didn't give me the internal validation I needed, I went for my balms of ruminating thoughts and comfort eating (aka self-sabotage).

What I wrote in my journal helped me see that what I feared was the ever-present reality that life would constantly be changing. I was focused on my professional transition, but life would have so many other uncertainties that I would not be able to avoid. I was doubting my ability to weather the ever-coming changes headed my way. I was scared. I just wanted someone to tell me they loved me and that it would all be alright.

And more than that, I wanted to feel the calm and peace that I'd felt just months back in February when I took the first steps into my new world. I tried to will back the thoughts, feelings, and lessons learned from my first ever solo-corporate retreat to return.

It was time to get to work on Dena Speaks, and I had no clue what that really meant. I could tackle operating a business, but before then, I had one big treat in store for myself. I had booked three nights away at Camp Comfort, a peaceful looking bed and breakfast in Comfort, Texas, that I'd dreamed of going to since I first saw it in a magazine years before. I would go and enjoy a solo-corporate retreat.

That's right, a corporate retreat for one, please. Businesses took their people, their boards, or their management teams on retreats all the time to talk strategy, plan programs, and build team camaraderie. I had been on several of these retreats before and loved the amount of work that could get done in a short amount of time. So why not take myself away for a few days?

It was a cloudy day, not even a week after walking out of the doors of what had been my work, and the views during the two-hour drive through the hill country were beautiful. I made my way to the property and found it easily, marked by a vintage canary yellow Ford Falcon Van parked right out front. I was the only car there.

I grabbed my things—suitcase, yoga mat, computer bag— and headed to my room. It was quiet and peaceful with a fire pit and chairs, a water fountain, and a creek flowing in the back. I was in love with all the little touches that made it feel comfortable and knew that following my heart and making this dream a reality had been an excellent choice.

Before I got lost enjoying the space, I checked my agenda. Because what's a retreat without an agenda? I'd created a daily schedule that struck a balance between rest and work, play and focus. I wanted to have a plan that was also flexible. And that is exactly what happened over the next few days.

I woke up, ate breakfast, did yoga, read my morning devotionals, and journaled. I set daily intentions and meditated. I worked on preparations for the launch party and my website. I went into town and ate at the local diner that was hoppin' with ladies playing cards. I soaked in the jacuzzi tub in the room, oh I don't know, maybe every other hour. And at night, I watched movies in bed or ate by myself out at the tables in the courtyard.

On the third and final morning, I was a little antsy like I am on all travel days but still not quite ready to hit the road. I finished a book called *The Big Leap* by Gay Hendricks and was repeating what he called the ultimate success mantra over and over in my head and out loud. The mantra was simple:

I expand in abundance, success, and love every day as I inspire those around me to do the same.

After wrapping up the book, I went straight to my morning journaling and noticed that a new sign had started to pop up in my life. In addition to seeing 5s all the time, now there were 3s. I knew curiosity wouldn't kill me, so I went online and found that the number 3 was associated with adventure, creativity, and humor. When 3s started to show up, the angels were trying to tell you that your prayers had been heard and that you needed to have faith in the Divine that your goals and dreams would be manifested in life.

Angel number 3 was significant because it's encouraging the one who sees it to grow emotionally, to be self-confident, and to communicate with others. It also said that the number 3 symbolizes abundance which was on its way.

Abundance, you say?

The morning's mantra came back to mind, and I repeated it out loud once more.

I expand in abundance, success, and love every day, as I inspire those around me to do the same.

I couldn't help but put it all together in my mind.

I was sitting in my room—Alley #3—on the *third* morning, reading of expansion and abundance. I took a deep breath in and let it out slowly, closed my eyes, and started my final morning meditation. I took the time to express gratitude, and like I had grown accustomed to doing, I silently asked all the parts of me this question: *Anyone have anything to say?*

I waited like I always did. Then, from what had to be my heart, I heard *three words* repeat themselves *three times.*

I love you!
I love you!
I love you!

I burst into tears and accepted the gift I'd just received.

I loved me. I knew I did. For so many years, I lived by my go-go-go mentality, and I had gotten going so fast that I couldn't hear or feel the energy inside me. But now, I had learned to slow down—to find time by myself. And I had finally heard the voices that I had longed to hear the most.

I love you!
I love you!
I love you!

I knew that I'd forever remember that moment when through my tears a smile full of hope and peace spread across my face. Camp Comfort would forever be a place that had given me what comfort meant: *to give strength and hope to.*

But I was ready to go home, to my family, and my work, and the life of my dreams. As I drove home, I smiled thinking of my daughter who'd said, "The best way to have a dream is to have a million." She was right! I had started dreaming again and had many dreams ahead of me now. So many things to create, so many lessons to learn.

And while I sometimes wanted life to slow down, or felt rushed by the need to produce, or became terrified because I didn't have all the answers, I was finding that my dreams would come to fruition in their own time. I just had to calmly and consistently chase them. So, I decided then and there to enjoy each and every moment. I would give each dream the care and attention it deserved.

I couldn't stop life from unfolding, and I honestly wouldn't want to.

I just had to hold on and enjoy the ride!

That was then. This was now. And I was back to feeling anxious and frazzled. But I had to get myself on steady ground. So, I prayed on it. I told JP about it. I shared with Janine, who had the best listening ears around. And when I shared my fears, they lost some of their power. I forgave myself for freaking out. I extended myself a little grace for the pizza pity party. I did my best to celebrate myself for taking the time to sit in what I was feeling, figure out what it was rooted in, and make a choice to pull myself out and on to a better path.

I might not have enjoyed the experience, but I had grown stronger for it. I had learned something from it. I had proven that I could change my course, choice by choice.

This was a lesson I'd have to keep learning, over and over and over again. Life is all about choices. I tell my kids all the time to make good choices so I'll have to practice what I preach. For me, the biggest choice I would consistently have to battle was whether I'd choose fear or love.

When I said the words, "I just know I am meant for more," I had no idea what that journey would look like. Naively, I imagined a life full of beautiful blue skies without a cloud in sight, me smiling and gazing lovingly upon all the good things in my life, healthy and thriving.

But what I had learned after taking the time to look back into my life and dig deep into my childhood, adolescent, and adult memories (while also dreaming forward of the days to come of course) was that the road of life is never without twists, and turns, and crappy pot holes. It wasn't meant to be easy. It's easy to get lost along the way. So many of us found ourselves asking the same question: *How did I get here?*

Over the years I had slowly but surely lost the love I had for myself. I had been directionless but decided to fight to get back on the road and feel the power of that love. My heart learned that once I could truly love myself, I would find myself. And then, I knew I would never be alone.

Not only had God created me and loved me unconditionally, God knew all the parts of me that I had to spend time getting to know. And once I had done that, I fell in love with all those parts of myself, too. I knew they would guide me as I ventured into the unknown with calm consistency.

Would I have to remind myself every day to love myself? Odds are, yes. Would I have to remind myself to be brave every day? Most likely, yes. Would I have to tell myself to slow down, look both ways, and then cross every new street with caution? Probably so.

Every single day, I would have to choose to love myself and stay brave. That's exactly how I made it this far! I followed my very own Meant for More way! I was my own proof of concept. I was living proof that I could make different choices that would forever change the trajectory of my life. I was living proof that I didn't have to have all the answers to take the next step. I was living proof that slowing down did not mean stopping my dreams. It worked; it really worked!

My Meant for More journey was and forever will be one of faith.

And it will be for you, too. Faith will be required because we simply cannot know what the future holds. I can't know for sure what will become of me or Dena Speaks, but I can be sure that I will stay committed to loving myself in spite of it all. I am proof that faith matters. I will hold tightly to it knowing that God and the Universe have a plan custom built just for me. I will take step by cautious step forward knowing that they will lead me to my next gigantic leaps of faith.

On top of faith, we'll be required to hold to hope. I cannot let despair or the fear that tomorrow will be just like today take hold of my heart. I cannot allow hope to be dimmed in my life.

And you can't either! We all have a light, and it wants to shine. Mine wants to shine a light for me to follow. To brighten the path for others, too.

But maybe more than faith and hope, we'll always need love. I will need to give and receive all the love that I can every day, to others, but even more so, to myself. That was the ultimate lesson of this journey: I have to love me! We must love on ourselves the way no one else can.

I will always have an immense amount of gratitude for the love and support of the people who stood by me, cheered me on, called me out, or texted me through every decision I've made. But that's just it. No one could have gotten me through this journey but me; it was a personal labor of love! I had to make my own decisions. I had to decide what kind of life I wanted. I had to do something to make it happen.

I had to love myself through it all.

And I'll have to keep loving myself because I haven't crossed the finish line yet. I haven't reached my final destination. I want to love and celebrate the fire inside of me, that heart and soul of mine that longs to be well and has stayed the course. I want to take a small victory lap for the person that I have become. My journey will continue, but I have to honor the voice that says: *Don't rush me. Stop and look how far you've come!*

So, that's just what I'll do. And it's what you'll have to do, too. You'll have to stop yourself from the race that is life and celebrate yourself. You will have to love on yourself. Tell yourself how amazing you are and find the warm pride that takes over when you know you've pushed yourself into something new. Does it feel strange? Sure. But you'll get used to it. I'll show you how easy it can be. I'll share a few parting words of love and affirmation with no one other than myself and pray that one day you'll do the same.

Wow! Congratulations, Dena! You did it. You kept going. You believed in your faith and your calling. You trusted yourself, your family, your friends, your strength, and your determination. You asked questions. You waited and listened for answers. You made choices. You were brave. You learned tons of new things. You felt all sorts of new feelings. You belly laughed and ugly cried. You ran into uncomfortable things instead of away from them. You allowed yourself to experience what it meant to heal.

You stayed committed. You challenged yourself and your limits. You trusted your gut, Dena, and you kept going! You worked so hard! Now, go get a vanilla chai and a cake pop! You deserve it. Take the time you need to rest, reflect, and reaffirm where you are headed. And no matter what, stay at it (whatever "it" might end up being). Keep going! Your work is not done. Amazing things are in store. I just know it!

I love you, Dena.
I really, really love you!

Conclusion

What's Next?

I'M DREAMING AGAIN.

I'm back at that same intersection. The lights are still flashing red. I still don't know exactly where I'm headed, but I know it's the road trip of a lifetime. It feels so different than the last time. *I* feel so different. Calm and oddly excited. There is a shimmer of pink off in the distance. The sun is rising. Pink is turning to orange, and it's breathtaking as it mixes with the blues and purples on the horizon. It's gorgeous. I hope I don't wake up.

This dream is getting good.

I can sense I have somewhere to go, so I better get my bearings. I'm buckled in. The car is on. I have the windows down, and a soft cool breeze is flowing over my face. I look to both sides and then check what's in front of me.

Open road.

When I take a final look back though, my heart starts to race. I get all hot inside, and my cheeks start to flush.

When did they get there?

This can't be happening, but it is.

Standing behind my car, just far enough back to create a semicircle of love, are all my people. JP, Trace, Elizabeth, my mom and dad, my in-laws and second set of parents that I snagged by marriage, my sister and brother-in-law, and my nephew and niece. My sister- and brother- in laws along with their significant others and their precious kiddos, six altogether. My dear aunts and uncle, Juanita, Marilyn, and Gary are right there behind them. They are all there smiling and waving.

My dear friends are there, too. Alisa, Janine, Sonja, Kim, Allena, Veronica, Brendan, Chandler, Sarah, and another Sara— they're all here. Next to them I can see Carri, Julia, Jules, and even Dr. Maynard all standing tall and looking so proud. I see friends that I made at work, friends from my community, and friends from back in the day at school. Old and new friends and family, they are all here to cheer me on as I hit the road. All the circles in my life have created one tight-knit community in this very moment.

I can't hold back the tears. Everything is blurry again, just like the first time, but not because it's dark or foggy. The tears are the only thing keeping me from seeing clearly. All of these people are here to wish me well. They are here support me just like they have done time and time again. They love me so much, and they have shown up for me!

I get my tears in check, but when I look back one more time, my heart feels like it might burst. There she is, all the way in the back. Smiling her sweet and sly smile, holding a huge sign that reads, "Keep Going, Deaner Weiner!" Of course, JoAnn would be here. She's standing next to Granny Cole, Mee Maw and Paw Paw, and Granny and Grandpa Lehman. They all look so happy, so well.

And just like that, I wake up. I'm so sad to see that dream go. But if I close my eyes, I can still see it. It might not have happened, but it's real. My brain has seen it, and now believes it to be true. I am deeply loved and supported; it's a fact. I have created the life of my dreams; it's true. Sure, I had to get lost in a couple of roundabouts, stuck going in circles until I could finally get out of that dang thing. Sure, I had to hit some dead ends, make some u-turns, and take countless potty breaks and rest stops.

But I made it.

Now what?

I can't just stop here. I have to challenge myself to consistently live outside my comfort zone. If I've learned anything over these last few years, it's that slow and steady wins the race—*my* race. Right foot, left foot. Right foot, left foot. Calm consistency is the perfect way for me to stay my course of fearless growth toward the life of balanced freedom I longed for. I must stay on track and on the road, ever creating the life of my dreams.

But what if life gets me down again? What if things get too hard, and I seek the comfort of complacency? What if I settle again? I've done it before. How will I keep from falling into that trap again? Well, this time I'll put into practice all that I've lived and learned.

First, I'll forgive myself and extend myself a little grace for being human. Then, I'll close my eyes and remember my dreams of a strong, healthy, and fulfilled version of myself. I'll repeat Proverbs 13:12: "Hope deferred makes the heart sick, but a longing fulfilled is a tree of life." I'll hold tight to faith, hope, and love as my guides. I'll look back into my mind's eye and know that I always have a crowd cheering me on, telling me to keep going.

Then, I'll look straight into the rear-view mirror and see that the one who matters most is looking me right back in the eye.

I'll tell myself, *God loves you and so do I!*

I'll take a deep breath, put on my sunglasses, and look up to realize that the light has always been green.

Fear may have stopped me before. But from now on, I will tell fear to hop in the back seat and ride with me, because it is time to go and grow! I will put my foot lightly on the gas and ease into the wide-open lanes before me.

Don't settle, Dena! Your heart and soul are and will forever be, meant for more!

But psst!

Hey you!

Yes, you!

Hey friend!

Did you think I forgot you were here in the front seat with me? Nice work! I'm proud of us—you and me. I hope you had as much fun as I did. I hope you felt things like you know I did. And most importantly, I hope you grabbed a few things that might help you as you chase your dreams. I can't wait to cheer for you on your very own Meant for More journey, and I will forever be grateful that you took the time to read about mine.

I don't want to leave you though without telling you a few things first. So, before you hop out, hear me please!

Your life matters. Your journey and all its different twists and turns matters. Your story and all its different chapters—they matter! You are going to have to get in your own way until you are ready to get out of it! You got this, friend! Keep going toward whatever dreams you have in your heart! You are meant for more than just living your life; you are meant to love it!

But if you ever have a day when you aren't feeling the love (which is normal and should be expected as part of the process), take my words and let them be yours. Let these words fill your mind and give you something new to hold on to. Because I believe these are just as true for you as they are for me!

I am brave.

I have bold dreams.

I am full of confidence and conviction.

And I will continue to grow, day in and day out, not only because I am capable, but because I know in my heart and soul that I deserve all that life has to offer me!

Be brave, dear friend, every day and in every way!

I'll see you out on the road!

Acknowledgements

THIS BOOK WAS A DREAM. One that I somewhat flippantly decided I'd make a reality. But it would never have become the book it is today without the love, care and support of some special people in my life.

To my first-ever Editor—Kat, thank you so much for meeting me back in 2015 in a small coffee shop and quickly embracing me and my journey. You were kind and patient throughout the process of birthing this book. You guided me from my laundry list of ideas, my self-debate on genres, through a muddle and mess of words, all the way to a finished manuscript. I will forever be thankful for your exercises that kept my newly found creative passions flowing. From writing character studies to walking the aisles of Barnes & Noble, you kept me learning through experience. Your consistent presence and belief in my story was a Godsend. Thank you for believing that I was an author from day one.

To my next level team of Editors—Ally and Sara, thank you both for meeting me and my manuscript in 2019 and being the exact right fit for its next round of love. I am thankful for the calmness and clarity you both brought throughout the process. You gave me just the right amount of instruction, guidance, and atta-girls. You believed in my story, and you believed I could find a way to tell in a way that was kinder to the reader (and by that you know I mean about twenty-eight thousand less words), and for that I (and the readers) are forever grateful. You taught me how to embrace the Delete key and to do my best to NOT overthink the process. Thank you both for huge lessons about letting things go—lessons that I will carry to my next book and to the rest of my life!

To my friends—Alisa, Janine and Veronica—You three ladies have supported me at a soul deep level. You each challenged me in your own unique ways while all showing me how much you cared. Thank you for the getaway weekends, reminder texts to breathe, and genuine smiles and hugs of love and support when I did my thing. You each hold a special place in my heart. I pray you know I am ready to return your favor of love at any time!

To my family—Mom, Dad, Peggy, Jimmy, Mandy, Richard, Blake, Kristen, Lindsey, Brad and all my beautiful nephews and nieces, Parker, Mallory, Tyler Bree, Riley, Blakely, Bennett, Archer and Dylan—thank you for being part of my family and loving me and my family without condition!

To my hubby and kiddos—JP, Trace and Elizabeth—I am honored to be a part of your lives. I pray that I show up as the wife and mother that you all deserve and that you know at the core of your beings how much I care about each one of you.

Thank you for supporting me through the years it took to get this book from the dream in my mind to the book you now hold in your hands. I love you all and am so proud of the family we are.

To God—thank you for being so unfathomable. You know I question how the world works and I'm thankful that you are open to my curiosity. You know I have had moments of doubt (and will have more in the future) and I'm thankful you still show up for me. Thank you for giving me the guts to slow down enough to see where I believe you wanted me to go. Thank you for giving me a unique passion and the courage to pursue it. Thank you for sticking it out with me and this book—I hope you love it! Thank you for making no sense and all the sense in the world! Love you, love me!

Thank you for coming!

I hope you enjoyed *Road to Hope*. To continue
following me on my journey, check out the fun
at denajansen.com. Hope to see you there!